to everything on earth

new writing on fate, community, and nature

to everything on earth

Edited by Kurt Caswell, Susan Leigh Tomlinson
and Diane Hueter Warner

Foreword by Bill McKibben
Introduction by William E. Tydeman

TEXAS TECH UNIVERSITY PRESS

This book is typeset in Filosofia. The paper used in this book meets the minimum
requirements of ANSI/NISO Z39.48-1992 (R1997). ∞

Designed by Kasey McBeath

Library of Congress Cataloging-in-Publication Data
To everything on earth : new writing on fate, community, and nature / edited by
Kurt Caswell, Susan Leigh Tomlinson, and Diane Hueter Warner ; foreword by
Bill McKibben ; introduction by William E. Tydeman.
            p. cm.
    Summary: "Collected essays on the nexus of fate, community, and nature by a
group of writers and scholars that have collaborated on several initiatives and projects tied to the same. By looking at external landscape and the human heart, the writ-
ings explore how to best make a home on earth"—Provided by publisher.
    ISBN 978-0-89672-655-0 (pbk. : alk. paper) 1. Nature—Literary collections.
2. Human ecology—Literary collections. 3. American prose literature—21st century.
4. American essays—21st century. I. Caswell, Kurt, 1969– II. Tomlinson, Susan Leigh.
III. Warner, Diane Hueter.
            PS648.N32T6 2010
            810.8'036—dc22

                                        2009032865

Printed in the United States of America
10   11   12   13   14   15   16   17   18   /   9   8   7   6   5   4   3   2   1

Texas Tech University Press
Box 41037   Lubbock, Texas 79409-1037 USA
800.832.4042   ttup@ttu.edu   www.ttup.ttu.edu

FOR THE EARTH, AND ITS MIRACLES

The real topic of nature writing, I think, is not nature but the evolving structure of communities from which nature has been removed, often as a consequence of modern economic development. It is writing concerned, further, with the biological and spiritual fate of those communities. It also assumes that the fate of humanity and nature are inseparable. Nature writing in the United States merges here, I believe, with other sorts of post-colonial writing, particularly in Commonwealth countries. In numerous essays it addresses the problem of spiritual collapse in the West and, like those literatures, it is in search of a modern human identity that lies beyond nationalism and material wealth.

BARRY LOPEZ, "A LITERATURE OF PLACE"

. . . countless silken ties of love and thought
To everything on earth the compass round,
And only by one's going slightly taut
In the capriciousness of summer air
Is of the slightest bondage made aware.

ROBERT FROST, "THE SILKEN TENT"

contents

foreword

I think Barry Lopez is right when he says, in the epigraph to this book, that the real topic of nature writing is human community. Questions of responsibility, of obligation, of possibility—the damage we chronicle in the natural world is usually the result of the extreme individualism that's come to define our culture. The only hope of "healing the earth" is first to take on the infinitely harder work of healing that community.

Which is one reason this is such a joyful book. It comes out of community—comes out of community twice.

In the first place, consider the band of nature writers. I've known many literary species over the years, watched them from my perch as a young man at the *New Yorker*. Ego, too often, is the defining mark, the characteristic flash of scarlet at wing's tip. That's *not* true with the nature writers I've known, who form an unusually tight and loving, albeit widely scattered, tribe. Partly that's because their work is more divorced from academia and big-time commerce than most writing, and hence a little removed from the universe of prizes and tenures and other competition. Partly it's because almost everyone involved is hard at work defending some place, and needs the help of their colleagues. (I'm spending the year helping to organize the first big global grassroots action against global warming—and the first people I called on to help were members of the fraternity, from Terry Tempest Williams to Wendell Berry to Michael Pollan.) Mostly, I think, it's because by definition nature writers spend a lot of time outdoors, and hence are reminded regularly that they are small. Ego is a little stunted by exposure to sky, wave, tree.

So it was unsurprising to get a call from Barry Lopez asking if I'd come to some dry corner of Texas for a few days and work with some younger nature writers. Barry Lopez is an elder in this tribe (morally, if not chronologically), and an exceptionally responsible one. He'd been working with Texas Tech for years, in defiance of every coastal convention about what constitutes an obvious location for such an endeavor. (Neither word, "Texas" or "Tech," sounds auspicious to a green ear.) But if Barry asked, I would of course come, as would Alan Weisman and Dennis Covington. And we were well rewarded. The town of Junction turned out to be the lovely kind of dry (and boasted, for sale in the parking lot, the greatest collection of deer stands I've ever seen). Not only that, but the collection of carefully selected writers that assembled for the workshop, most of them young, was equal parts talented and enthusiastic.

And, more to the point, they were up to the task of community. Not only for the few days that we spent along those sandy washes, but in the years since, when they have stayed in touch, shared drafts, and worked together to produce the volume you hold in your hands. It includes many works of great individual power, but that is not its highest beauty. What makes me happy is that this book grows out of community and hence points toward the real solutions. Writing involves ego, necessarily—the conviction that what you've got to say is worth others hearing. It cannot be any other way, just as our modern economic life demands a certain kind of ego. But allowed to run amok, it is that ego that spoils the planet and spoils literature too. These stories and this experience point in a different, older, more durable direction. If there's going to be writing for a sustainable planet, this is what it will look like.

BILL MCKIBBEN
Ripton, Vermont

introduction

Dennis Covington, Barry Lopez, Bill McKibben, and Alan Weisman sat on the stage of the outdoor amphitheater. It was the first outdoor session of our October 2004 gathering, "Writing the Natural World," at Texas Tech University's Junction campus in the Texas Hill Country. The earlier morning talks were informative, interesting, and prepared with care. I thought they demonstrated the imaginative possibilities of utilizing science in the service of community. The participants seemed to agree. I was relieved.

In the open air I listened for bird calls. I hoped to hear in the oak and pecan woodlands behind the amphitheater the black-capped vireo. Thirty-six nesting pairs were reported nearby in the state park along the South Llano River. I caught a glimpse of a black phoebe moving through the underbrush toward their foraging areas along the clear waters. But the words of the speakers soon concentrated my attention. I thought of Reg Saner's line, "fresh air keeps language alive." As I listened to first Barry Lopez and then the rest of the panel, I thought back to the conversations with Barry in the months preceding the gathering. The panelists, in their own words, mirrored our earlier discussions of objectives. My notes from these conversations contain the following statements, each on a separate line filling the page:

> The celebration of self in nonfiction often leads to social
> irresponsibility.
>
> Western culture's decision to separate from the natural world
> creates the conditions for intolerance.
>
> The 21st century is dominated by information, not narrative
> structure.
>
> We lack a dependable narrative structure.
>
> Stories remind people, without indictment, how to behave.
>
> Storytelling is an ethical obligation.

And finally, on the next page of my notes, not a declarative sentence
but two related questions: How can we be of service, and do these
stories help? In retrospect, I came to better understand, in both
formal and informal conversations, these questions provided a
structure, a touchstone, for the issues we discussed over the two and
a half days we came together at Junction.

The last question, so eloquently expressed in Spanish, "¿En qué
puedo servirle?" or How may I be of service? was not only the ani-
mating principle for much of Barry's works, but the central precept
for the "Writing the Natural World" gathering. As Barry and I talked
we realized our workshop models, our notion of "best practices,"
were similar. His influences go all the way back to a conference
organized by Stephanie Mills in 1981 at Mills College entitled
"Crossing the Invisible Line." There some one hundred people came
together to prepare presentations, listen to each other, share their
work, and ask for help when needed and support. The writers created a community, kept in touch, and shared perspectives. My model
was the Orion Society-sponsored conferences, most recently "Fire
and Grit" in Shepherdstown, West Virginia, in 1999. As with these
gatherings, we wanted a flexible format with a few experts; we would
invite a few known writers and experts in related disciplines to provide information for a group of writers, perhaps less well known; we
wanted to create a sense of fellowship and common cause that would
help create work in the service of community. In retrospect, I was
looking to reify the "Fire and Grit" experience. I wanted to tran-
scend the petty resentments of academic culture, to escape from
colleagues who regard themselves as better than others; I wanted to
reinforce the service relationship where we are the servant of talent

rather than the talent others must serve. Barry once cautioned me "to respect scholarship but avoid its tyrannies." What we found in the writers at Junction was the practical wisdom and grounded observation present in story. These writers use narrative to tell stories that force us to remember what we have forgotten, to look back on our own life and recognize significant moments of transformation and change.

Ten years ago, when I first came to Texas Tech, I was attracted to the strength of its biology field programs, to the lack of pretension among the senior faculty, and Tech's determination to become a major research university. It is still a secret to most of the academic world, but today the university possesses the finest collection in North America of contemporary writers of place: the James Sowell Family Collection in Literature, Community, and the Natural World. It includes the personal papers of Rick Bass, Max Crawford, David James Duncan, Gretel Ehrlich, Edward Hoagland, William Kittredge, John Lane, Barry Lopez, Walt McDonald, Bill McKibben, Susan Brind Morrow, Doug Peacock, David Quammen, Pattiann Rogers, Sandra Scofield, and Annick Smith. Tech now offers support for researchers in the form of Formby Fellowships for one to three months working in our collections. Each year an internship is available to an English graduate student to assist the Sowell Collection librarian in processing new additions and making the collection more accessible. A lecture series is in place where we can encourage presentations that address the cultures and communities so far underrepresented in the collection—Native Americans, blacks, and Hispanics.

Texas Tech University also boasts one of the finest field biology programs in the world—a program old-fashioned enough to incorporate the observation and practicality of traditional fieldwork with modern molecular biology. The Natural Science Research Laboratory collects tissue specimens worldwide. Former president David Schmidley said back in 1999: "Texas Tech has the best field program in natural history research in the country. It is the best program in mammology probably in the world." The biologists are field smart, practical, and widely read.

The final piece in this program was the development of the

Natural History and Humanities degree program (NHH), an inter-disciplinary undergraduate degree housed in the Honors College. It is one of the few undergraduate programs in the country combining competence in field sciences and mastery of a humanities discipline. Inspired by Barry Lopez and E. O. Wilson, and designed by a team of faculty and administrators at Tech, the program (like the Junction gathering) emphasizes that the scientific method is but one way, not the only way, of knowing. Empirical or real experience combines with imaginative inquiry.

The Junction gathering, "Writing the Natural World," was a programmatic extension of these emphases. However, the idea for a workshop was Barry's. After agreeing to place his papers at Texas Tech, Barry began to serve as the university's first distinguished visiting scholar. He comes to campus twice a year to meet with classes, conduct readings and lectures, advise students, and assist in developing programs. He enriches the intellectual life of the campus in leading a faculty seminar, meeting with writing students, and supporting the NHH program. So when he asked, "Why not provide some support for up and coming writers who share a vision of the importance of literature in the elucidation of nature and culture?" I jumped at the chance.

We looked for practical ways to structure a program with activities that a group of emerging writers could use immediately to aid their research and writing. We decided on practical, yet flexible sets of interactions where writers could get to know one another early on and, we hoped, continue to communicate and support each other after the conference. Thirteen writers accepted. Texas Tech paid the housing and meal costs, and waived all workshop fees. The writers paid their own travel expenses. As speakers we sought out senior writers Bill McKibben, Alan Weisman, and Dennis Covington of our own Texas Tech University faculty. We thought it wise to include editors and publishers. H. Emerson Blake, then of Milkweed Editions, and Dan Frank of Pantheon agreed to join us. We debated the bugaboo issues of gender balance and ethnicity, worrying that while we had a number of women as participants we were less successful with speakers. And of course, in the absence of African Americans and Native Americans we were subject to the usual critiques of nature writing as a white middle-class preoccupation dominated by writers from the West. We took some satisfaction in reminding ourselves that, outside of the gathering, we intended to invite Comanche people to return to their homeland on the Llano Estacado and participate in the life of the university. With the help of our Hispanic faculty, we identified future speakers and contributors who would help diversify the Sowell Collection.

The writers invited to the workshop would share their techniques and approaches. They prodded us to think harder about how a university might extend itself in the world, how we might nurture the shared ground of science and the humanities. In addition to the speakers, writers, and editors already mentioned, we invited Bill Rossi to share his understanding of Thoreau and his enduring importance. On the science side, Kent Rylander, Texas's leading ornithologist, spoke on the scientific concept of fixed-action patterns (FAPs) in birds, managing in less than an hour to give us the latest science on instinctual behavior. Kevin Mulligan, director of the Center for Geospatial Technology at Texas Tech, wove a tapestry of points, lines, and surfaces to explain the overlay process of digital cartography. Isabelle Sterling, director of the Science Library at the University of California at Berkeley, opened the first afternoon with an informative introduction of open-access Web-based research tools.

The writers who attended the conference and whose essays make up this anthology were chosen through referral and recommendation. Barry and I talked about writers with first books or essays that helped propel us toward a more civil and just society. Barry wrote letters and made telephone calls to editors, publishers, and other senior writers. We made lists; we wrote the writers. We also decided to include writers who work in Tech's Southwest Collection/Special Collections Library and the NHH degree program. In the end, after writers expressed their excitement (and some in turn suggested other writers), we came up with people whose work fell into a range of expression that Barry often talked about: a unified demonstration of the approval of life, work free of dogma that helped us to answer the question, "How do we take care of each other?"

As I read this collection of essays, I am reminded about the

changes in writing about the natural world since the celebration of
the first Earth Day. The essays in this anthology, like today's writing
on the natural world, cover a wide range of experience. The choice
of subject and theme extends beyond the traditional bounds of
nature writing to issues of social justice, the fate of our children,
and the nature of community. In fact, the label of nature writer has
little utility in a collection this diverse.

As a central theme, I'm also struck by the degree to which these
writers go beyond observation itself to demonstrate the concern and
insecurities of what has been called "the vulnerable observer."
While several essays fall within the traditional concerns of writing
toward home (and the learnings that accrue from becoming one
with the landscapes of home), all these essays seem to elucidate the
emotional connection between the observer, the observed, and the
reader. Amid the range of vulnerabilities expressed here, we come
to see the mystery of nature's healing.

In *To Everything on Earth* we come to know and identify with the
writers through their insecurities and fears, their pain and joy. They
become our companions. The vulnerability expressed here serves to
remind us of the shared responsibility that we, as individuals in a
larger community, face. Opening the window to our wounds helps us
recognize the healing properties of nature. Such stirrings of the
human heart require new ways of imagining the relationship
between the individual and the natural world. For me, this is a collection of new and better stories—stories that engage both the ethi-
cal and moral dimensions necessary to build a culture of trust and
hope. Herein is the power to illuminate and make sense of our own
lives.

WILLIAM E. TYDEMAN

to everything on earth

from the ground

MARYBETH HOLLEMAN

From the air, Nunivak Island looks as lovely as I'd imagined—
curves and swirls of varying shades of green, the tan arc of a shoreline, and steel-blue water, it too swirling in shades of itself.
Mekoryuk, the only village on this island in the Bering Sea, tilts
into view as the plane bends toward it: a small boat harbor and a
compact oval of buildings clustered along the coast beside a river's
mouth. Closer, I see what must be the school, biggest building in
town, and a thin straight line of road emanating from the village and
out across treeless tundra to the gravel airstrip, where we land.

We walk the narrow dirt road. A wooden skiff sits on blocks, listing
toward sunlight. Upon one roof, a walrus skin is stretched to dry,
and next door, the fuzzled head of a musk ox sits in a weathered
wooden skiff. Spaces between houses blossom with useful objects—
fishing floats, four-wheeler engines, blue tarps, piles of salvaged
lumber. In the fields behind the houses, five pale yellow umiaks sit
upside down on blocks, like a pod of beluga whales surfacing in a
green sea.

   A woman walking by on the other side of the road crosses over
to say hello, reminding me that in this village of 215 Cup'ig Eski-
mos, thirty miles offshore of Alaska's Yukon-Kuskokwim Delta,

three visitors—especially three tall, blond, Caucasian visitors—do not go unnoticed.

"Are you," she says, slowly, "are you here on vacation?" It's said kindly, but incredulously. No one comes here for vacation; there are no hotels, no tours, no facilities for visitors. My husband, I tell her, is here for work, and my son and I just came along.

"Oh, why?" she asks. I forget that this island—the high volcanic plateaus across which herds of musk oxen and reindeer roam as on a northern Serengeti, the wide sandy beaches, and two-hundred-foot-high cliffs where thousands of seabirds nest—is just, to her, home.

I answer briefly, saying something about wanting to get away for a while, or I tell her the truth: I've wanted to come to Nunivak Island since I first read about it twenty years ago, and I want to show my ten-year-old son, who has lived his entire life in the city of Anchorage, how some other Alaska kids live.

I've come seeking a better comprehension of the urban-rural divide, the apparent rift between the 60 percent of Alaskans who live in cities and the 40 percent who live in the Bush—mostly in Alaska Native villages much like this one.

The term "urban-rural divide" was first used in the late 1990s, and now it's everywhere, in speeches, reports, newspaper stories. One report describes it as a "cultural fissure" caused by "conflicts over education funding, access to health care, tribal governance, and land use."

Adult concerns, adult words; I've lived and worked in Alaska long enough to know these inequities are real. Interviewing the Tlingit residents of Kake about their subsistence use, I saw them clam up and slam their doors in my face, out of fear and anger that I might be there to constrict their hunting and fishing. Reviewing the juvenile detention records of Village Public Safety officers in the Cup'ig villages of St. Michael and Stebbins, and the Aleut village of St. Paul, I recognized the absurdity of applying federal laws created in Washington DC to these small, intimate villages. I'm no stranger to the myriad ways in which village life clashes with city life, but my experiences all preceded the waves of debate and discourse about the urban-rural divide.

I wonder how it is now, decades later. How prevalent is this cultural and racial schism on the ground, face to face? How much is imagined, or created, or magnified, in the too-busy minds of adults? Knowing that ignorance of each other's lives feeds this fissure, I want my city boy to have at least some unmediated ground truth of life in a village.

It's just a glimpse he'll get, only in town a few days in June. My husband, Rick, is helping fishermen with their longline fishery, a relatively new foray into a cash economy for this mostly subsistence community, a commercial enterprise that doesn't easily weave into the weight and heft of their daily life, the rhythms of fish camp in late summer, reindeer roundup in fall, seal hunting in winter.

James loves everything about this place, immediately. He loves the one-room house we get to stay in, sleeping on cots on a linoleum floor, the tiny space heater, the raised compost toilet. He loves the dirt roads with 10 mph speed limits and only two trucks, no cars, where kids can drive four-wheelers all over town, on any road. "They don't need a license?" he asks, more than once. He loves the dogs that roam throughout town, especially the little red short-legged one that looks like it's part red fox. What he loves, I think, is a kind of simplicity and freedom that city life often lacks.

We stop by Oscar's Originals, an art studio, and the only shop in town besides the grocery store and fuel station; inside there's a boy exactly James's age. He's playing at a computer. Good, I think, they have something in common; maybe they'll play together. But Aaron is quiet, and barely looks at James.

Not an hour later, we're walking across the tundra toward Mekoryuk River, and Aaron runs up behind us, falls in step with James. "Let me show you something," he says, to everyone or just James, I'm not sure. Aaron runs ahead, so easily across the hummocky land, and we follow clumsily, down to the bouldered shoreline where the river rushes by, dark and deep. Aaron and James throw stones, skipping them over the water's ridges. Then Aaron says, this time most certainly to James, "Let me show you something," and they scramble down the shoreline. Heading back toward the village, Aaron whispers to James, "C'mon, let's ditch 'em."

* * *

At the village offices, the manager and assistant spread before us a
hand-drawn map of their island, showing the river's curve out to
sea, the bird cliffs, the volcanic peaks, their fish camp. They urge us
to come back and take a boat to the northwest cliffs to see auklets,
or east where the musk oxen spend summer. I imagine kayaking
those shores, encouraged by their eagerness to show us their
island's charms. I love especially the lilt in their voices when they
talk about fish camp. I'd already noticed it in Aaron's voice, as he
told James, "Oh, you have to come back for fish camp!"

Night, it's late, we're all settled onto cots, inside sleeping bags.
The door flies open and three boys burst in—Aaron and two others.
"Where's James? Can he come out?" Tomorrow, I say, tomorrow he
can play with you. I'd forgotten that, in these villages in summer,
people follow the light and not the clock. It's still light outside at
midnight, so it's not yet bedtime. Some nights they may not sleep
at all.

Walking across the field just beyond town, in front of me are six
children: James, Aaron, and Aaron's brother and sisters. They are
taking us to the beach. "We want to show you something," they say.
The two oldest girls, Kayleen and Caroline, run ahead, then run
back and give me two bouquets, one from each—wild geraniums,
lupines, asters. They run ahead again, this time to pick wild celery.
"We eat this," they tell me, their eyes wide and bright. Up ahead,
Aaron and his brother Jeremy have taken off their coats and are
crouching and walking forward slowly, coats over their heads like
sails. They are stalking a pair of wild ducks walking in front of them.
Look at this, I say to Rick, these children playing at what the
adults do—hunting and gathering. Subsistence training.

We all climb up the dunes that tower between the fields and the
beach. The boys run, jump, slide down, clamber back up quickly, on
sand that is soft and warmed by midday sun. We walk across dune
tops, sea breeze whipping the long dark hair from the girls' pony-
tails. Holding my hand, they bring us to one hilltop and show us the
gravesite of their mother.

They talk about her easily, but I don't ask the question I think of first. She was young; what did she die of? Village life contains such different dangers: alcohol taking so many Native lives, boating accidents in Arctic seas, snowmachine strandings in winter storms. Perhaps it wasn't the dangers, though; perhaps it was the difference in health care between village and city.

The children would tell me, if they knew, or wanted me to know. I don't ask; I just hold their hands, and listen.

We slide down the dunes to the beach. It's wide and flat, hard-packed golden sand backed by the dunes that, like a small mountain range, hide us from the village. Here and there, rock juts through sand, flanked by swirls of tidepools. The older kids organize a game. Rick is the referee while I hold Emily; she's only three, and her legs have tired out. Or maybe she just likes being held. Or maybe she knows I like holding her.

The race begins at one rock outcrop; they run barefoot to the row of their rubber boots, pull on their boots, and run back to the starting line. Aaron wins several times, but the third time he stops to help James get his boots on, so James is a close second. Fourth time, one of Aaron's boots fall off and Caroline wins. Then the game deteriorates, or transforms, into tidepool splashing.

Rick and I walk back to town, leaving the kids playing on a huge sand mound, one they've built up into a kind of fort, playing king of the hill. When I last looked, Aaron was on top, Kayleen was climbing one side, and James was scrambling up another, laughing.

Late at night, there's a party at our little house: eight kids sitting on the floor in a circle, a pile of comic books and some snacks in the middle. Two of Aaron's friends have joined in. I stand in the doorway, watching all of these children leaning over the pages, reading to each other, laughing. The next day, James leaves some books with them. "They don't have a bookstore," he tells me.

From the plane, I see children, the ones who showed us their island, playing on the mountain of sand. I'm glad they were so friendly, and say so to James. Then he tells me something that Aaron told him on the second morning. One of Aaron's friends had asked him, "Why are you playing with that fucking whitey?" Aaron told James he'd answered, "I just want to."

My smile freezes as I tumble through anger at Aaron's friend, sadness that a child could feel that way, gratitude to Aaron for not being swayed by his friend, worry over how this might affect my son. I churn through what I might say to soften the harsh words, to keep my son from feeling the sting of racism, and from harboring any seedling of racism himself. Should I tell him about the urban-rural divide, about the social and economic differences between Native village life and his city life? Should I tell him the history of Europeans and Native Americans? Should I have waited until he was older, or knew more, before bringing him here? Should I try to explain the friend's hatred, or protect James from it?

All I say is, I'm glad Aaron did what he wanted to do. For, after whirling through my own fears and hesitations, I notice the way James told me about it: in a light, matter-of-fact tone, as if he was relating the color of Aaron's four-wheeler, or the size of the sand mountain. No need to add weight to the words.

Home, I get pictures developed, and sift through them looking for one of James and all the kids on their front porch, one I'd been looking forward to seeing, to sending to Aaron's family, sharing with them—they were all so sweet. There's a lovely close-up of little Emily in her pink coat, sitting on a sand dune; another of Aaron and Jeremy climbing up the sand, barefoot; and another of all the kids running on the beach, a jumble of boots at one end. But when I reach the porch photo, what strikes me, first and foremost, is how, standing among those lovely Mekoryuk children, my own son looks so startlingly white. And what most astonishes is not his pale skin, but how all I'd seen when I was there, on the ground, taking the picture, was a group of joyful children gathered together.

working the stone

Peter Friederici

Then dusk came and the color faded like a dream that was hard to hold in
memory. The exhilaration that this image induced, though, persisted
through the next day's travel, and the one after that, and it became easier
to see how the nomads could refer to the desert as Allah's garden without
being ironic. Austerity and serenity intersected, and the emptiness was
not empty at all, but pregnant with meaning.

A'Yóba understood the feeling, he said, and approved.

Marq de Villiers and Sheila Hirtle
Sahara: A Natural History

Bare rock and sand and nothing but blue skies: deserts may
seem marginal places to our production-oriented, get-up-and-go
civilization, but in fact the emptiness of the desert lies at the core of
Western culture. Consider: Egypt was not a desert—at least not the
cultivated part where Pharaoh ruled his people. It was a linear oasis
hundreds of miles long. Regular and predictable floods flushed
down from wetter lands, enabled productive farming. It was a land
of vegetables. There were leeks and onions and herbs. It was the
regularity and abundance of the water, and of the food supply, that
made a centralized society possible, perhaps inevitable. It was hot
and there was no rain, but this was no desert.

They may not have known it, but what the Israelites sought when
they fled was exactly the desert. They escaped the hydraulic society
and the rigid hierarchies of the Nile along with its oppressive ruler,
and wound up in a literal no-man's-land of burnt mountains and
parched earth. What they needed was a place governed not by
humans but by God, and the only such places were those so barren
and worthless that most people wrote them off. They found just that
in the crucible of the Sinai, where, it is said, only the intercession of
God assured them enough food to eat and water to drink.

Some wanted to turn back, even at the cost of returning to tyranny. It is always tempting to trade independence for security. But the freedom of the open sky and the hard land did their work. In a country lacking a rigid social structure, the Israelites were free to forge a new society and a new religion. In a place of little water and food they learned to rely on one another as desert dwellers must. In a land of silence and space they found that the absence of the sounds of humanity allowed them to hear the voice of God unalloyed.

In the Sahara there is a saying that Allah retained the desert as a place without extraneous life so that he might have one refuge, at least, in which to walk in peace.

The Israelites did not stay in their tents forever. At length God showed them the way to the Promised Land, which proved to be a more fruitful place than the Sinai. And things went on from there. But the desert ever and always was the place of birth. It was the liminal place where the old order was destroyed and a new one created. It was the place where they learned who they were, and how to ask the right questions, and how to pray.

After the desert, everything was new. And it had all come out of nothing, out of hard rock and bare ground.

Something coming from nothing: it is the central riddle of the Bible as it is of high-energy physics. Maybe it is because the riddle comes most easily to mind where there is little stuff around that the desert has so often and so easily become the home of mystics and religious hermits.

This at least is what I find myself thinking one long week in May. I am conducting bird surveys in the burnt-looking hills and gravelly flats of Arizona not far from where the Colorado River debouches across the Mexican border, corralled by dams and irrigation outlets, and disappears into the flats of dried mud. Every morning the sun climbs a bit higher into alabaster sky, and every day the temperature rises to and exceeds 98.6 degrees a bit earlier.

I can tell when it does. In the afternoons my colleague and I take refuge under a big ironwood tree in our camp where a large, gravelly wash pours out of a low and parched mountain range. Below 98.6, shade still makes a difference: one can seek shelter, imbibe cool drinks, rest comfortably. Yes, it's hot, but in an ordinary way. But

when the ambient temperature exceeds that of the blood there is no
longer any way to escape. When we move, we sweat. We breathe, we
sweat. Our bodies are surrounded by heat the way a cooked noodle
is surrounded by its bowl of soup. It's full immersion. The heat is a
heavy weight. I lie still, but even so the sweat runs into my eyes. A
wind picks up—there is always a wind in the hottest afternoons—but
it is a hot wind that offers no relief, merely sucks the moisture out
of any flesh and blood in its path, stripping any coolness from the
shade. When the temperature rises above 98.6 I feel the blood
pounding in my vessels as if it were expanding and trying to escape.
It races and pulses, trying to carry off the excess heat, but there is
nowhere to take it. So the heat rises until it is too hot to move and
there is nothing to do but wait.

The heavy light of early afternoon bears down on the landscape,
flattening it into bright white. I am exhausted by the heat, sopped as
a wet rag, marinating in my own juices, but there is no way to sleep.
There is time, lots of it; the birds are not active in the afternoon; we
have little to do. The heat pulls us into ourselves and conversation
dies away. We measure words out as if each one were made of ice
water. There is ample time to read, but in the desert I cannot read
lengthy books. This is not a country of long tea times and Russian
novels. This is the land of the epigram. And so every afternoon I
pick up a slim volume on the early Christian desert fathers who in
the fourth and fifth centuries AD went out into the deserts of the
Negev and the Sinai and spent their lives there. The book is by
Thomas Merton, who throughout his career had so extraordinarily
much to say about brevity, about silence.

"If these men say little about God, it is because they know that
when one has been somewhere close to His dwelling, silence makes
more sense than a lot of words," Merton writes. "The desert had no
contribution to offer but a discreet and detached silence."

This was not true. In the great age of the Christian monks and
hermits, the desert had much more to offer than that. It was out of
the reach of the secular authorities. It had a great number of
canyons, cliffs, caves, and other natural features that could be converted into remote but sheltered monasteries or hermitages. It had
just enough scattered water sources. The climate was tolerable: hot,
to be sure, but at night and in the winter generally not cold enough

to require overmuch clothing or shelter. And, yes, it was quiet and relatively unpeopled, though the widely dispersed Bedouin had lived there since biblical times or before. In the Middle East, the desert was simply the best place to get away from the noise and hullabaloo of civilization.

Some went because they found themselves unable to live in the cities and towns and villages. Some went simply because they were fleeing the tax collector. Some went because Jesus himself had spent forty days in the desert resisting the temptations of the devil. Some lived in monasteries, some alone in isolated hermitages. Some stayed put in solitary caves for decades. Some went on walking pilgrimages forty days long, finding the food they needed in the charity of others or, so it is said, through divine intercession. They drank water from springs or collected the runoff from rare storms in stone cisterns. They ate simple bread and beans, foraged on wild greens and saltbush. Some grew a few vegetables. Those who were educated turned away from the learnings of the secular order. Many withdrew from the bright world and sat in small caves all day long, day after day, praying and fasting. They renounced possessions, in some cases even their Bibles. They exercised silence and patience, week after week, month after month, decade after decade. Outside their cells the hard white light was a hammer striking the anvil of silence, and in those vast spaces they heard the desert ring.

Like anyone, they endured temptations. Demons appeared: sexual desires, gluttony, self-righteousness, sloth, ego, even fame. Some of the hermits became celebrities, of all things, and had to move farther out into the desert to avoid the crowds of admirers and followers who wanted to shortcut their own route to spiritual freedom. Many faced the greatest temptation of all, that of feeling so buoyed by their discipline and asceticism that they thought there must surely be some easy shortcut to the enlightenment they sought.

The proper response to the demons, the elders counseled, was silence, forbearance. "Any trial whatever that comes to you can be conquered by silence," says one abbot in Merton's book. Or: "It is said of Abbot Agatho that for three years he carried a stone in his mouth until he learned to be silent."

Lying under our tree, sweating as easily as we breathe, we are quiet as monks, but the desert is not. The wind blows hard and the twigs and branches clatter and gnash. Dust flies. Sand grains have blown into my mouth and eyes. I drop the book and close my eyes. The afternoon seems endless. The stones under me are hard. I lie still and wait and it seems there is nothing to hope for, unless it's next winter, or the next visit to some air-conditioned building that will seem shabby and antiseptic and far too cold after a few minutes. Even the coming night, with its blessed shade, seems far too far off to be an event that will take place in this same world. And so I wait. There is nothing else to do.

The blood pounds, the chest rises and falls with its mindless exhalations, and soon there is nothing left to wait for. Soon the future becomes an abstraction that is more a curiosity than a genuine destination. It's like looking at the moon's surface through a telescope: fascinating, yes, but not a place I can imagine myself leaving any footprints. And so after a spell on a superheated afternoon, there is nothing anymore but the present moment, nothing but the flimsy shade of this ironwood tree and the buzz of some audacious bee and the breeze that rustles the sand grains. There is nothing but this breathing and sweating and this hard pressure of the body on its bed of earth. Maybe an ant crawls by, or a vulture wings overhead, curious about this unmoving mammal of the desert floor. So patient, as Edward Abbey wrote, but only *so* patient, and ready for whatever opportunity it finds.

At such a time it does not even disturb my equilibrium to know that a vulture has good reason, here, to hope for a good meal at the end of a trail of footprints. Not in the middle of a hot desert afternoon.

Some of the desert fathers went out deliberately, as Jesus did, to meet their demons, to prevail over temptation. Think of it: no weapons, a social structure stripped to its barest essence, only the most basic food and drink and clothing and shelter; no protection against whatever demons chose to present themselves other than a silence extracted like the purest homeopathic essence from the word of God, which, in turn, drew heavily from the silence of the desert. Some, it is said, went on their walks without water, trusting in God to provide. They themselves were as bare of superfluities as the desert they trod. They strove to be as humble as the desert was dry, as bare as the rock walls of their hermitages. Maybe that unity was what moved so many to give up so much.

Even on a long desert afternoon I cannot imagine myself into the mindset of the fourth century, but in the heat I can begin to imagine what some of the demons they faced may have been. In our modern culture, certainly, there is nothing more frightening than shedding all the shields that we carry around with us, from the literal armor of our cars to that of our telephones, our computers, our hectic schedules, our social obligations and to-do lists. The heat presses down on the desert and on us and it is as if its weight were enough to squash out the past and the future, leaving nothing but the immanent moment. It is as if some hull were removed, a muffling membrane of whose presence one is scarcely aware until it is missing. The body becomes so very intimate with its surroundings, fully engaged. It is bound to the heat by sweat and by the breath. The body opens to the desert, the desert to the body, but it is a pitiless opening. There is no way to escape the present, no way to escape the immediacy of one's bodily situation. Eventually there is no need to do anything anymore. No way, either, to ignore the massive indifference of this harsh environment to one's presence. The rock is hard, very hard. On a hot afternoon it is all too apparent that the weight of the present could easily be enough to squash one's very life out, and that this act would mean nothing, absolutely nothing, to the desert.

But even the threat of death is less frightening than this shedding of the past and the future, this coming face to face with the immediate present and with the stark reality that it is in this moment, only this one, that I truly know I am alive, and that because of all that stripping away of the armor of civilization I must acknowledge at last that I am alone in this as in every moment. This is living: right now, that's all, says the heat, the emptiness. The mind rebels against this. Maybe this is what the desert fathers found: in the desert, with so many superfluities stripped away, they were able to—*had to*—come face to face with the demons that came

from inside. In the severe invocation of the present they had to con-
front their own true selves, which in every cultural setting is a
shameful, embarrassing, fearful act.

I have not prayed in the desert. I do not believe in the burning
bush. I have not let a stone do the talking for me, or seen the angels
descending in glory. And yet on an endless hot afternoon I do find
myself, after a while, feeling an affinity with those hermits of long
ago. In giving in to the present moment, I can accept the pure
immediacy of being in a way that transcends the daily problems of
life and the fears. I can even accept my own eventual death, if I work
at the giving-in—though this is an odd sort of work because what it
really means is loosening up, relaxing into the world, like falling
back into a really comfortable chair. It is a matter of not striving all
the time, of not struggling—what? to get ahead, to be known as an
individual, to earn more, to set oneself apart, to fight just as a matter of being human.

Perhaps this relaxation is not unlike the final settling into death,
into the cessation of all responsibilities, even the responsibility to
breathe. Perhaps desire is the final layer of armor to shed. The
stone in the mouth says: Just be. Just be here. That's all.

What's the payoff of all this time in the desert, the time all those
seekers spent so many centuries ago, the time I've spent? Nothing,
I'd say, nothing at all. Isn't that wonderful?

I cannot claim much wisdom here, only the certitude of knowing
that somewhere in the desert, where the superfluous is stripped
away, there is such wisdom to be found. And so on a hot afternoon
all the stuff I can think of clatters in my brain for a while—names of
birds, descriptions of the particularities of their habitats, thoughts
of what I will do when I finally return home, concerns about my
bank account, about politics, about friends. It clatters around, and it
clatters away. Under the ironwood branches I can feel all the junk
rattling through, and away, and eventually I can forget it all. It's like
the alluvial gravel heaped up on the slick bedrock underlying the
wash, waiting for and needing a good flood to wash it out and clean,
bare, ready to start over.

That's a good image, I think, lying there. Abbot Agatho would like it. Perhaps he would nod in approval, his tongue silently working the stone. I could write about it. Now, better to forget it, too. So I lie there and the sun declines toward the west and a black-throated sparrow sings its high tinkling song and it's the most beautiful sparrow song ever, nothing but itself, pure.

homeland security: safe at home in the world

SUSAN HANSON

It is morning as I walk along the bare caliche road, as my sandals crunch across the gravel, drowning out the mid-September songs of birds.

It is morning when suddenly it occurs to me that, for reasons unexplained, I am not being struck by lightning. I am not falling into a crevice and disappearing into the earth. I am not bursting into flames or whirling into space. My body is intact.

It is a morning in mid-September when I wonder why it is that I so seldom marvel at the fact that I'm alive. Why does it seem so ordinary to be occupying time and space?

I hold out my hand and see the veins, see the knuckles, tendons rippling underneath the skin. I see the tiny scar there on my middle finger where I accidentally burned it as a child, the callus where I gripped the pruning shears too long.

What is it, I wonder, that tells my hand to brush the bangs out of my eyes, that tells my fingers to adjust the glasses riding down my nose, that tells my feet to rise and fall, rise and fall in a rhythm that makes sense?

As a rule, I must admit, I am not moved by mysteries such as this. And yet, *this* morning I am baffled by them all. *This* morning, for an instant at least, I am fully in my body, fully in my life. My feet are on the ground. I am, as some would put it, "placed."

Were I more literal-minded than I am, my curiosity would not be piqued by such phenomena as this. I would be satisfied to know, for instance, that it is some electric impulse coursing down the nervous pathway from my brain, some charge emitting from any of 10 billion neurons causing me to stop on this caliche road, to bend over from the waist, to touch the flower of an Indian mallow in full bloom.

As it is, though, I'm confounded by the simplest of things.

Think about it: The earth is traveling through space at something like 67,000 miles an hour, the galaxy at more than 370 miles a *second*. Though I state these numbers as I might recite my zip code or my street address, I can fathom neither speed. Tell me that the average human body contains roughly 50 million *million* cells, that each of these cells contains six feet of chromatin—structures composed of DNA and protein—that *any* sequence of DNA in *any* complex of chromatin in *any* cell can go terribly, terribly wrong—wrong enough to kill. Tell me that my body is as vulnerable as this, and I will wonder how I've made it through a single day, much less the half a century that I've lived.

And yet, the truth is this: no less than the elbow bush growing wild outside my study window or the white-winged doves cooing at sunset, no less than the armadillo that roots in my garden at night or the Gulf fritillary that flits across the blooming flame acanthus— no less than any of these, I am suited to this place. It is my home, my source. We are a perfect fit.

This doesn't mean, of course, that real dangers don't exist. A coral snake might be hiding in the leaves around my air conditioner, just as one was when the repairman last came to do some work. The mosquitoes that nip at my ankles and calves might carry West Nile virus, or encephalitis, or something more exotic like, say, dengue fever. The ground beneath our house might shift, leaving the foundation cracked and all the pipes askew. The weather might turn bad. Hail, lightning, floods; "blue northers," tornadoes, ice—the possibilities for disaster are vast.

When I was growing up on the central Texas coast, for example, hurricanes were an indisputable part of life. Most of the time they skirted Bay City, where I lived, but in September of 1961, the strongest storm in forty years came inland across Matagorda Bay, the brunt of its power felt by the towns of Port O'Connor and Port Lavaca—only fifty miles away.

What were the odds of a major hurricane hitting so close to my hometown? In a typical year, fairly small. While tropical storms *are* endemic to this part of the state, the chances of one becoming a hurricane and actually doing serious harm are between 3 and 4 percent.

I suppose it was simply our turn.

With steady winds of more than 150 miles an hour and an eye that stretched for thirty miles, Hurricane Carla was a Category 4 on the Saffir-Simpson five-point scale—"extreme" by any definition of the word. Still the largest Texas storm on record, with its mix of hurricane and gale force winds cutting a swath five hundred miles wide, it produced storm tides of ten to twenty-two feet, left shrimp boats marooned on highways miles from any dock, swept up birds in the Yucatan and dropped them like hail on the Port Lavaca streets, or so some residents said. It spawned twenty-six tornadoes, removed eight hundred feet of Gulf shoreline from Matagorda Island, and cost forty-six people their lives—most by drowning.

Granted, there had been more *deadly* storms, such as the so-called West India hurricane that flooded Galveston in 1900, taking between eight thousand and twelve thousand lives. There would be more *costly* storms as well, including Hurricane Celia in 1970. This storm, with its wind gusts of almost two hundred miles an hour, would result in nearly half a *billion* dollars in losses to property and crops—the equivalent of $3 billion today. It would destroy close to nine thousand homes in the Corpus Christi area, with another fourteen thousand suffering major damage of some kind.

Yes, there had been worse storms, with a good many more to come. But for me, Carla was unique: The life it affected was mine.

Just ten years old at the time, I didn't know where to begin preparing for such an event. How long before the wind started, I wondered. Would our house be okay? Would *we* be okay?

Longing to do *something*, I rummaged through the kitchen drawers for a piece of string, went outside and, under the gathering cover of gray, tied a newly planted live oak tree—our *only* tree—to the street sign a few feet away.

I truly believed it would help.

My parents, meanwhile, stocked up on bread and milk, bought extra batteries for the flashlights, filled the bathtub with water—and tried to prepare for the worst.

Then, for as long as we could, the five of us—my brother, sister, parents, and I—watched a trenchcoat-clad Dan Rather broadcasting from the Galveston seawall. Gathered around our black-and-white TV, we sat enthralled by the sight of waves crashing over rocks, wind bending trees to the ground.

When the blackout finally came, my sister and brother and I went out to the garage and climbed into the front seat of my mother's 1957 Plymouth Fury. There we listened to the radio, periodically running back inside to give our parents the latest news.

The storm passed sometime in the night.

The next morning, with the water and power still off, we piled into my father's company car and headed downtown, where a single café was open and serving food. Coming and going, we gawked at the fallen trees, at the piles of limbs and other debris strewn across people's lawns. Among the lucky ones, we had lost only five shingles from the roof of our newly constructed house. To my parents' great surprise, the live oak had survived as well.

I was more than a little relieved.

Today, forty-plus years after this storm, I live on the Balcones Fault, the part of Central Texas where the Coastal Plains and the Edwards Plateau intersect. With its spring-fed rivers, limestone canyons, and oak-covered hills, it is among the most beautiful places on earth. It is also among the most dangerous.

Thanks to rapid runoff and the tendency for large storms to stall here for several days, no area in the United States is more prone to major flash flooding than the Balcones Escarpment of Texas. In late June of 2002, for example, as much as two to three feet of rain fell in only a matter of days. At Canyon Lake, roughly twenty-five miles to our west, the lake level rose forty feet, coming over the spillway for the first time since the dam was built. In the nearby community of Sattler, where flood stage on the Guadalupe River is only nine feet, the water crested at thirty-seven.

The upshot of all this? The earth is a dangerous place.

As a person whose house has been struck by lightning and whose bedroom window has been smashed by tornadic winds, I should probably be very afraid. Knowing what I know—not only about weather but also about rattlesnakes hiding under logs and brown recluse spiders nesting in people's shoes—I should probably shudder at the hazards of being alive.

I think of this now as I check the headlines or watch the evening news: earthquake in Algeria, SARS in China, tornadoes in Missouri and Kansas. Anxiety levels are high.

As much as we fear such natural processes, however, we fear ourselves even more. The threat of attack by terrorists is high, we're warned; the nation is on orange alert. As a result, citizens should be wary of anyone behaving in an odd or suspicious way. Assume that weapons of mass destruction, including those containing chemical, biological, or radiological agents, are being readied for attack. Though we can't know where or when, trust that terrorists are at this very moment planning to wreak havoc at a public event near you. Remember that the enemy is no one and everyone, that the danger, though amorphous, is real; it is like the air you breathe. Know that people with more information than you believe that the worst is possible—if not today, then tomorrow, or maybe a week from now.

The message? The world is out to get you. Be afraid.

Like many of my friends, I find little reassurance in the color-coded warnings or the airport screenings or the presence of men with guns. The threat is too fuzzy for these to appease my fears. *The times are dangerous*, we are told repeatedly. *Take care. Watch out.* But watch for *what*? we ask.

Life is out to get you. Be afraid.

Lying awake in the dark, I spent countless childhood nights imagining the way the world would end. First there would be a burnt orange glow on the horizon, then a blinding light, then the cloud. It could happen any night, I continually reminded myself. It would surely happen at night.

My fears were stoked not only by my choice of reading material—books such as *On the Beach*—but also by the duck-and-cover drills we did at school, by the fallout shelter frenzy, by images of a somber JFK addressing the nation and a maniacal Khrushchev banging his shoe on the table to drive a point home. "We will bury you!" he had warned us in 1956. His words hung in the air like smoke.

The atmosphere is much the same today. But with roughly 19

million Americans suffering from an anxiety disorder of some kind, we're now learning the price of our fear. We are learning the damage that hypervigilance can do.

Should we be concerned about possible terrorist threats? Only the very naïve would say that the danger's not real. There *are* malevolent forces at work to destroy the things we hold dear. There *is* evil in the world. There is cruelty and anger and the misuse of power. There is arrogance, intolerance, and greed.

I can't deny these exist.

At the same time, though, I can't live a life fed by fear. Just as I can't go to bed every night imagining a nuclear blast or a tornado tearing off my roof, I can't begin every day envisioning the worst things that people can do; I can't survive in a world where stopping to rest, to breathe, to be caught off guard, is seen as a perilous act.

So for me, the question is this: How *do* we live with the fear, with the awful awareness that we are indeed vulnerable creatures, that we face a risk that is real?

What the earth tells me is that the question isn't new. There has *always* been an inherent threat in simply being alive. A single-celled organism can fell even the strongest among us; a hundred-year flood or a tornado at just the wrong time can wipe a community out. People *do* lose their lives. In the mathematics of mortality, it's the way the universe works.

And yet, for all the precariousness of flesh, we are fundamentally safe here on earth. Given all that *could* go wrong—tsunamis washing away our homes, sinkholes opening under our feet, asteroids crashing on our heads—it's worth noting that such disasters are simply not the norm: They're still considered *news*.

There is, then, a kind of holding-in-tension that I am trying to learn. In this both/and way of looking at the world, security lies somewhere *between* the knowledge of our own fragility and our sense that we are at home here. To live with both truths is not to deny our fears, but to see them as part of the whole. Life and not-life, hope and not-hope—the capacity for paradox is what saves us.

"In this wilderness I have learned how to sleep again," Thomas Merton wrote in *Raids on the Unspeakable*. "I am not alien. The trees I know, the night I know, the rain I know. I close my eyes and instantly sink into the whole rainy world of which I am a part, and the world goes on with me in it, for I am not alien to it."

Several years ago, a friend who had been seriously ill wrote to tell me of the changes in her life. "I have the sense that I'm being distilled," she explained, "simplified by forces I can't name."

The process, she added, was less disturbing than it seemed. It was, in fact, a little bit like being on the bottom of the pool, or underwater in a lake, looking up and seeing the turbulence on top, but not being battered by the waves.

When I read this, I felt myself swept back to an afternoon just fifteen months before, to a moment when, having crashed into a massive rock, two friends and I were thrown from our canoe. While they managed to cling to the fallen pecan tree that was partially blocking our way, I was trapped beneath it, pinned down by the swirling current.

At first I was simply surprised. We had made a mistake, I realized; we could certainly make it right. But then the panic set in. Struggling to grab hold of the tree, I fought the weight of the water, fought the force that was pulling me down. *This doesn't happen to me*, I protested. But it *was* me, and I knew I was going to drown.

Life and not-life, hope and not-hope. In a split second, my world became quiet and still. With the sky a mere shaft of light above me, a blue glow in the midafternoon, I felt the fear slip away like a skin. For that moment, for *just* a moment, I felt safe. Living or dying, I was going to be okay.

Minutes later, *years* later, I had somehow washed up on a gravel bar, had dragged myself to a nearby rock, had sat there staring at my hands. What struck me then, what struck me later as I read the letter from my friend, was just how strange it was to be alive. Moved by the fact that I was still in my body, I had come out of the river knowing something that I hadn't known before. I had learned, quite simply, just how thin the margin between life and death really is. I had learned a little bit of letting go, of letting myself be borne away by something I could neither understand nor tame. I had learned to trust my own life.

"Everything *is* distilled," I told my friend, recalling the events of the summer before. It's distilled to something that feels like a single pebble or a single grain of sand or a single drop of water, and you know this "something" is your life. For an instant, you hold it in your hands or taste it on your lips, but then, quite suddenly, it's gone.

Walking along a rough caliche road in mid-September, a woman is jolted by the mental image of herself alone on a gravel bar, staring in amazement at her empty hands. *This is your life,* the stones in the river tell her. *Pick it up and hold it lightly; turn it over and over; let it go. Let it gently fall into the flow of the river. Let it be carried away like sand. Let it disappear from sight, becoming a part of the current as it goes. Let it not matter any longer that you have lost it. Let the losing of it set you free.*

Walking with the wind against her back, with the sun on the side of her face and the sound of crunching gravel underneath her feet, the woman is grounded in this time and in this place. She knows that the world is dangerous, that life is dangerous, but she also loves the way her body feels as it travels across the earth. Holding both hope and fear in her heart, she is, she knows, safe at home.

in the slipstream

LISA COUTURIER

> A man's work is nothing but this slow trek to rediscover . . . those
> two or three great and simple images in whose presence his heart
> first opened.
>
> ALBERT CAMUS

One day a strong goose came into my life. She arrived at the
wildlife rehabilitation center where I was working wrapped in one
of those blankets stained with oil and the smell of gasoline and left
in the corner of car trunks for situations just like this: an injured
animal found along a road and brought in, illustrating that there are
concerned and caring individuals living in the suburbs, and that we
do get out of our cars. Still, the journey of an injured animal is not
announced with ambulance sirens. There are no families scurrying
down a clean white hall behind a doctor steeped in Ivy League
degrees. A sick or injured wild animal, unless it is a baby with siblings or a mother with young, is catapulted into the human world all
on its own. The familiar feel of forest floor or grass, tree bark or
water under foot or paw is replaced with metal bars, wood and wire
walls, yesterday's *Washington Post*, and a heap of hope that something
can be done to save the animal's life.

When the Canada goose showed up at the rehab center, I was on
my hands and knees, buried in the cage of another goose (or gander,
it's impossible to tell the difference from feather coloration) that
eventually would be set free but was now paddling about in a
portable blue plastic pool while I cleaned its cage. The new goose
was making quite a raucous calling, and it quickly became obvious
that her personality was like that of the other geese residing at the

center: pissed-off, which is not a peculiar way for geese to be. Her fierceness, though, was of a different ilk, and for an entirely different philosophy, one might say. Her chance to bite the hand that fed her hadn't yet occurred. She hadn't done time in the metal cages or been harbored in the plastic pool that the other geese begrudgingly waddled to in the morning and refused to leave in the evening. Actually, these goose activities would have been, had she known such events existed for her captured kin, reasons for her to argue the good argument. Instead, she was here to fight the good fight, which, I believe she knew on some level, was a fight for her life: She was the goose who would not go down.

The long black velvet neck of a Canada goose is a neck designed especially for probing deep, murky waters. It is a neck that, when stretched straight during steady and tireless flights of up to sixty miles an hour over the earth, is the great identifying characteristic for those of us watching awestruck from below. It is the neck that was now swinging to and fro, side to side, an unleashed garden hose with the water turned on. The goose hissed. Her wings flapped as though she may have thought she was still flying over the fields that edge the multiplex movie theater where there is a pond in which vast numbers of Canada geese gather. Did she know that pond? Had she flown from that refuge and set down on the shoulder of a road, and been sideswiped?

Absurd as it sounds, some people go out of their way to run over suburban squirrels. And it may be the same with geese, most of which, in the urbanized East, no longer migrate and, increasingly, no longer hold a significant place in our hearts. Geese are permanent residents, having noticed the auspicious opportunities associated with suburban sprawl: vast manicured lawns of assorted business campuses; large, cleared public park lands; and an abundance of urban people, like myself, who hunger for that which is wild. Hunger, though, works both ways. What is tossed out to geese as a gesture of love—Cheerios, Pepperidge Farm Goldfish, bread crust, and empty ice-cream cones—has contributed to the drastic decline in popularity of the birds, whose inefficient digestive systems cause them to continuously excrete on the public suburban grounds where they once were welcomed but are now considered, by many, pests.

Though it once would have been a strange occurrence, it is now commonplace to see Canada geese highway hopping as they travel from man-made pond to man-made pond, or to see them contentedly poking around in the purple, red, and bright orange wildflowers that grow so well, albeit so incongruously, in the grassy median strips of multilane roads stitching together the suburbs of Washington DC. I admit to having considered stopping in these strangely peaceful highway strips; I have desired such surrealism myself. Could this strong-willed goose now be thinking of flowers?

I figured it could have been otherwise. An injured and frightened bird could go down, it seemed, in the face of such struggle. But her large and powerful heart, with the same basic design as the human heart—one that efficiently segregates oxygenated and deoxygenated blood, which, for her, made all the rigors of flight possible—kept on. Other animals let go more easily. The box turtle whose shell and body had been sliced by a lawn mower and resembled the latticed crust of cherry pie; the snake that slid into the bicyclist on the road and whose body was wounded into the shape of an exclamation point; the little brown bat—these animals went down. Some of the creatures I fed one day would be gone the next: the nestlings secured and sleeping in wads of toilet paper in the heated, white, dresserlike drawers; the newborn gray squirrels—their tiny paws kneading like a kitten's against my hand—whose eyes never would open to the world waiting for them. Working at the center required a uniform of sorts, a coat of toughness or a dress of death, both of which I uncomfortably squeezed into when necessary.

Until this goose, upon whose arrival nothing could be pinned together, nothing fit. She landed in my life with her daring heart that would not stop; and in so doing joined the elusive geese flying in the open skies of my thoughts: geese in all the months of one's life that come before, geese one senses in the months to come, geese in dreams, in memories, in the autumn air blanketing the cornfields. Witnessing her struggle, I felt her grip on something that of course I could only imagine—March winds in her feathers, splashdowns in green waters, arenas of endless clover, flights under fuchsia-colored evening clouds. And it was perhaps because I believed she longed for these things, or that her heart did, that I felt a headlong rush of images of my father, whose heart, unlike hers, had, for a time, stopped.

* * *

The phone rings about a parent, a relative, a friend who has had a heart attack. It is a call that tells a literal story: This person who has inhabited your life, who has sat with you in silence, walked with you in the rain, this person with whom you've shared meals, with whom you've been to the mountains or to the ocean, this person was at some certain place, on a sunny or a cloudy day, and in the moments when you were cutting the lawn or grocery shopping, working, or studying, suddenly, or over time, even, there was pain that slowly anchored in the body, or came on violently. This pain was the heart talking, or attacking, either or both, depending on perspective. This person has survived and is in the hospital, or this person has died. Clearly, the heart has successfully besieged the body that is its home. If death has not come, questions brew about how to fix this dying heart now thought of as a weakened heart, which it literally, physically, has become but which it may always truly have been—such as a lonely heart, a sad heart, or an open heart that was too open. And so it is decided the heart must be cut, bypasses must be made, when it is possible to imagine these, in part, could be reasons the heart initially shut down: a cut and wounded heart, a bypassed heart.

The surgery is said to be routine. Papers warning of possible death are signed and soon enough the knife slices the chest. Layers of the body will be peeled back. Ribs will shine through, be broken, and split apart. If such a scene could be witnessed, seemingly incompatible nightmarish images of the arched ribs of a great whale's skeleton might pass through the mind, along with the relentless ache to see the whale—its wonderful and generous and intelligent body—alive again. Wherever there is blood there is the clotting memory of moving through life with this person, this gentle whale of your life.

The hours sitting in the greenish gray waiting room tick by, and terms like *mitral valve, graft, cardiac pulsations, echocardiogram, coronary arteries, vascular system, right ventricle, angina,* and *coronary thrombosis* float in the conversations of the doctors and nurses streaming in and out of peripheral vision. Random facts from hospital FAQ sheets are remembered: a heart that beats tens of thousands of times a day; a heart like a gasoline pump, propelling blood not by cup or pint but by gallons into the tank of the body. At rare times, all of this slips into the mind and makes sense, somehow, as though it is what is known of the heart that invites us into it, rather than what is unknown.

"Ye need not go so far to seek what ye would not seek at all if it were not within you," wrote Emerson. Geese: how do they enter? Despite knowing the truth, since it could have been any suburban animal—a squirrel, a robin, a worm—it might be that geese were the first wild animals in me, my earliest glimpses occurring as a toddler standing at the edge of a suburban pond throwing breadcrumbs and french fries to these birds that, back then, truly migrated into and out of our lives. Years later, at seven, fifteen, eighteen, even at twenty-two and just before moving to Manhattan, season after season, geese were instructive in the idea of waiting. I want to say there's nothing I wouldn't do to see once more the geese in New York City. They threaded through the skyscrapers and over the Metropolitan Museum of Art, on Fifth Avenue, on their way to the reservoir in Central Park, which for the birds' arrival got all gussied up in sashes of red, orange, and yellow fall leaves. A walk through the park then was like snuggling into a gigantic autumn-colored sweater.

And what of the geese in the Arthur Kill marshlands alongside Staten Island? The ingenious pair who came upon the shore of Prall's Island and found what could be equated with a Donald Trump-like real estate discovery: an old black car tire. It was a tire affording an open view of the Kill and, across the Kill, a dead-on view of the lime-colored New Jersey wetlands, including all the circular, white oil storage tanks that resemble the Guggenheim Museum across New York Harbor and up Fifth Avenue, near Central Park. Having fallen off one of the many trash barges passing this way, perhaps the tire could be put to good use. But first things first. Before the goose could lay her eggs, before she could imagine leading goslings through the small and dirty waves left in the wakes of oil tankers motoring by, she had to construct a nest inside the tire. So as the gander kept guard, the goose stood in the center of this tire and began gathering the necessary material within her reach: cattail leaves from the marsh, sticks, reeds, and grasses. A mere four hours later, with the nest nearly made, the goose plucked soft, satin-like feathers from her breast and padded the cup of the nest with these gifts from her body.

I wonder how, on a summer day, when the heat of a city marshland sucks all your muscles into the mud and when sweat trickles along every inch of your skin, anyone could not be tempted, as was I. Tempted, since the goslings had departed and the nest sat empty, to rest my head on this pillow of a goose nest. It's not impossible to envision beginning every day from this island, this place where a goose and gander wake to the sun over the Atlantic before flying off to Central Park, the Metropolitan, the Guggenheim. But it is unfair to claim these thoughts, these desires, these imaginings, these experiences, without mentioning my father, who, if he has not loved any certain goose, has loved something about them and has passed it on to me.

I am home from New York for a visit, and, on the December morning that I carry my crippled dog into the cornfields, I awake to the wild barking of foxhounds and random gunshots ringing through the air. A goose? A red fox? Deer? Since I was sixteen and my father moved my family thirty miles northwest, away from the denser suburbs just outside of Washington DC, to the croplands and woodlands of Maryland's Agricultural Reserve, I have associated the sound of shotgun with the cold, with the crunching of dry leaves and the scent of chimney smoke. I didn't know then that there were hunting schedules—certain days, weeks, months for certain animals—or that the government wrote reports about the abundance of Maryland's wildlife:

> Maryland's citizens are fortunate to reside in a state that consists of a sequence of physiographic provinces that tend to bisect the region in a series of northeast/southwest swaths. Each of these regions represents interdependent physical and geographical features that influence the structure and distribution of ecological communities found within them. As a result, wildlife species and ecosystems representative of large portions of the eastern United States can be found in Maryland.

Put simply, this means there are lots of animals to hunt.

A goose is a resource, as is a piece of corn; and the harvesting of animals is executed with firearm, muzzle-loader, bow and arrow, or leghold trap. Have an urge to get out and run, chase, harass an animal? It is legal; be our guest. There are considerable choices available for those whose interests tend toward rampage and killing. Meanwhile, other citizens live with the sometimes surreptitious, yet deep, desire simply to glimpse geese, mink, river otter, coyote, opossum, raccoon, skunk, long-tailed weasel, fisher, beaver, nutria, muskrat, even bobcat.

When I arrived for this visit home, I dreamt of a reacquainting ceremony for my old, dying dog. And now, on this windy day, I will set her down in the frozen soil of brittle corn and hope she remembers her runs here and the way it was when we waited with my father for the passing of geese. It will be cold, and I am looking forward to the clear Maryland air, to the way December dives into the body, surging down the throat like so many invisible diamonds.

There have been innumerable Decembers before, when snow drew my father into the drifts to build igloos, sleigh, and play games like "fox and geese," a traditional snow country game that we called "mouse and dog." One person is dog, the hunter, and the others are mice, the hunted. Renaming the game to "mouse and dog" happened over time, as our dog—who, before she was crippled, relentlessly chased but never caught either dozens of actual mice or one very intelligent mouse—demanded her place in the moot hunt. The fun of the game was switching between one heart and another, dog into mouse, mouse into dog, and all the concealment, deception, and goofy fury that went with it, as though the animals did such things.

Even so, the sound of barking and gunshot in the air made it impossible to forget that beyond our game were actual foxes and geese; and, against my father's wishes, I remember trying to follow the sound of the gun with the falling of a goose from the sky. It was then, when I was looking for death, that my father turned me toward the birds' lives. If, as the geese hit the sky above us, they were not in full V formation, my father pointed out their elegant assembling until there was nearly perfect equidistance among them all, with one goose, usually a mature gander, leading at the tip of the V. He explained the theory that when the geese trailed one another in their formation each goose encountered less air resistance and thus saved energy. It was known as flying in the slipstream, each bird's flight assisting the bird behind it, a force that drew the geese together through the sky. Though he also questioned if this sharing of energy might be thought of as one energy. Imagine, he said, watching them fly farther west, toward the green waters of the Potomac River. Eventually, the lead gander would fall out and another bird would take its place. What could that be, he asked, breaking out of his reverie, but a flock with one brilliant heart and many souls?

Still, questions of the hunt lingered. Which animal was fleeing in which province? Goose, deer, fox, mink, river otter, skunk, opossum? Unlike my game of mouse and dog, these animals did not switch between identities, did not become "other," though I've heard now that such things are said of hunting. Things like the hunted comes to inhabit the hunter, through some sense of the animal's compliance to surrender, or physically, later, through the eating of the animal's body—the validity of either being known only to those who've taken the shot.

Where was the hunt, and the witnesses? Some seasons, these questions were partially answered, when foxhounds, followed by men on horseback, men dressed in absurdly colorful formal jackets, stampeded through the nearly one thousand pines on our property in search of foxes clearly still alive but nonetheless running like ghosts of themselves, invisible and exquisitely fast entities attempting escape.

With all this, it should not be surprising that a dream recurs, inconsolable, as though it is a dark anthem meant to recompose the waking life, but never does. And so a goose comes again to me in the night. She falls into my dream's pale field, into the sounds of the dogs in packs, crying, yelping. A river of red spreads over her body, while the sky slowly sips away the surviving birds. I cradle the goose to my chest, autumn's yellow wind preening her. What is a goose's life but cold stories of broken ice below her body in winter and memories of warm thunderstorms punishing her flights up the wild spring water? The goose in my dream is dying beside forest fringed black with crows, dying under skies stitched with the hissing of rhapsodic vultures. I must snap the neck of this bird thrown down into these hollow hills, through which, I sense, the goose and I soon will fall. Then the season abruptly changes, and it is spring and times of light blue flying. Still, the goose is suffering on my lap. The hounds are coming, or going, when I wake up, unsure of what has happened to the goose.

After night, it is morning, and again I am convinced my father has brought me to a land of immense loss and confusion. It is my sense that I never kill the goose in my dream, though it would have been the merciful thing to do.

I remember my dream goose again when, in the one-window post office run by the Mennonite woman, I say hello to the hunters who hand me a pen while licking stamps; I think of the goose when a hunter offers up his seat to me at the ice-cream counter in town; the goose flashes across my mind when hunters, breaking to buy lunch, help me with groceries in the old wood-floored market too small for grocery carts. Season after season, hunters dressed in camouflage park their trucks in town. We meet face on, and I hunt for what I'm meant to say: That with them here the rest of us live in the crosshairs of cruelty? What? Something my grandmother drilled into me plays over and over: "Be kind, for everyone you meet is fighting a great battle." And so there is altogether everything and nothing in how we leave it: "Thank you."

In these wide tracts of earth absolutely drenched coral by sunset, where disappearing is possible, where if you stayed out long enough your hair smelled like wild grass, and where geese flew in slip-streams of other geese, skein after skein, my father, the dog, and I, year in year out, reckoned with the indefinite things entering our hearts.

There is a definition for a completely unpronounceable word belonging to the Yamana natives of Tierra del Fuego, in Ushuaia, Argentina, and the definition, according to the Yamana-English dictionary printed by the Reverend Thomas Bridges in 1933, is: "to be light, not yet dark, to be a little light, light in the sky, as before day light and after sundown." It is almost like saying something is beautiful, or almost beautiful, though not ugly. Or saying something is complex, though not terribly complex, but not simple. Ideas within ideas. Contradictions. Layers upon layers. Lives within other lives.

These are the things, I think now, that my father intuited could be taught me by this land, where woods met fields, where sky met earth, where new houses met old farmhouses, urban folk met rural folk, and where, while calling to geese, I met my father and began piecing together the layers of him.

In Maine in the late 1940s, the boy that would become my father lived, sporadically, in a white clapboard cottage with an outhouse, in patches of neglected soil carved out of the forest. Back then, children were less considered than today, and so uprooting, relocating, shuffling a boy between Maine and the projects of Boston and New York City, was, it seems, a normal part of the child's breaking, like a horse. Unsure of an alcoholic father's return, and existing long periods without a mother, the boy rambled through provinces of abandonment. A few faded black-and-white snapshots of the years in Maine reveal a boy both haunted and hunted by loss—always a slight smile, a looking away or through—as though loss can prey upon a person. "It is a deep mystery that love is born in the mind's (and body's) experience of emptiness and loss," writes Belden C. Lane in *The Solace of Fierce Landscapes*. "The longing of the soul, made sharper by the painful absence of that which it loves . . . reaches in darkness for a beloved who comes unannounced and without guarantee."

And thus geese enter, geese as distraction, as company, as my father's beloveds, mysterious and elegant, traveling overhead on the Atlantic migratory pathway to and from their breeding grounds in Canada. And so, too, enter stray dogs and forest creatures and the birds he loved most, blue jays. I remember him telling me, when I was a child, the story of how he stalked blue jays. Their vibrant color drew him. For hours he tried outwitting them, attempting and often failing to lure the jays with suet into cages he'd fashioned out of twigs and twine. The few birds he caught he stood by, admiring them, speaking to them, feeding them. Soon, he freed them. This is how, I believe now, my father became a man made of birds and trees and why, when we moved to our field in Maryland, he planted nine hundred pines, one hundred dogwoods, and twelve pear trees, creating, essentially, a forest for himself, and for me. A forest that called in the animals—hawks, crows, mice, opossums, foxes, blue jays, robins, owls, chipmunks—the creatures that lived on the slopes of his heart, evidently long ago bypassed in childhood.

Jung said, "We are forever only more or less than we actually are," which is an idea much like the Yamana word about light— things as more finely layered and intricate than what is actually seen. I am thinking, then, of my father as a boy with blue jays, as a boy stitching together not only twigs and twine, but a torn heart, a heart lured by the wild creatures we hunt because of both our passions and our battles. In stunningly simple yet complex moments, all those many years ago, a boy and his blue jays, or his creatures, or his geese, intermingled over and over, rising and falling, dipping in and out of what my father sensed even then was one brilliant energy—one heart with many souls. This was where, as a boy, he played: in the slipstream of animals.

And so it has come to this, to the idea of being forever only more or less than we actually are, which, in my father's understanding of the world is forever only more or less than a blue jay, or the geese migrating overhead, the geese in New York City's wastelands, or the insignificant geese in the pond by the movie theater. Of being forever the hunted fox sprinting through pines, the deer hidden in fog-covered fields; of being the strong goose who came into my life and died later that day, finally, peacefully, with her great wings folded against her like the closed petals of the flowers she loved. This is my father's legacy.

shadow gods

JOY KENNEDY-O'NEILL

The Almighty blesses you
with the blessings of the heavens above,
blessings of the deep
that lies below,
and blessings of the breast and womb.

GENESIS 49:25

It is the day before Christmas. White frost still sprinkles the ground where the yellow sunlight has not touched it, patterning the town with clearly lined frost-shadows of its houses, porches, and eaves. The telephone poles are decorated with large wooden cutouts of frozen-smiled nutcrackers. It is early; there is no one else on this small town road. Something black and lithe moves from the sidewalk to the street, running in front of me as I tap the brakes. A tail disappears in the hedges. A black cat has crossed my path. Today, of all days.

I arrive at the hospital still bleary in that cold half-sleep that comes from early morning appointments that you wish you didn't have to keep. The gown feels like wearing an oversized paper towel.

"Now, where is the lump?" the technician asks.

I point to a spot on my right breast, a spot that holds a tiny, one-centimeter secret—as round and as hidden as a pearl.

2001, Belize
Marcos shoulders the rope and adjusts his helmet light. "The jaguar god is the Mayan god of the underworld: Xibalbá. During the day he was the sun god, but at night he entered the caves and returned to his cat form. He would paddle through the water caves to the other side of the horizon, where he would come up again as the sun."

"What else would he do?" I ask.

"Many things," Marcos shrugs. "He was the god of life and death. Some say that the unrolled skin of a jaguar is the night sky and stars."

We are waist deep in water in Waterfall Cave, in central Belize. Like the jaguar god, we too have entered through one entrance and will exit through another, a half-day's hike away. Will we come up on the other side of the horizon? Will it be dark, and will the skin of the jaguar be the stars?

Walls encrusted by quartz glisten like diamonds in my helmet's light. Always, there is the sound of water moving. I've been caving for nearly a decade, but I've never seen sights like these. In shadowed crevices are broken pots and burned spots from the smoke of incense, long ago snuffed out. There are obsidian blades, small and sharp as razors. The Mayan priests would have pierced their tongues, genitals, and ears. Thorny cords would have been pulled through the bleeding holes. Blood was collected and offered to the gods here. Women would not have been allowed in such sacred places, for as with many world cultures, the Mayan thought the ability to menstruate made them unclean.

But I am here. Now. Whole and unbroken, strong.

I pull the gown aside and point. The technician stabs roughly at the spot with a ballpoint pen, which won't write on my skin. A few more jabs produce an inky X near my nipple.

"Take your right arm out of the gown."

I do as I am told and she positions my breast between the plates. The mammogram machine clicks as the plate begins to lower. It is a behemoth of a machine, almost elegant in its sheer monstrosity. It is six feet high and the color of all sterile offices: off-white, eggshell, ecru, biscuit-bland.

The technician positions me carefully. "Arm here, hand on this, this shoulder back, this shoulder forward." I am a bare-breasted mannequin. I am a ballerina frozen in first position, waiting for X-rays to bombard my cells.

She is all business, with no idle talk. The radiology staff is looking forward to going home early in just a few hours. Visions of sugar plums and who knows what else are dancing through their heads.

Not cancer. Certainly not thoughts of me. How can I tell her that the arm she is positioning pulled me up a cave's waterfall? How can I tell her what these hands have felt? *"You are skinny strong girl!"* After the cave, Marcos had fed me termites and shook my hand. Can I ask her if this woman's body is now rebelling against me? She wouldn't know. She knows nothing about me, except the age I started my first period and that I have had no pregnancies.

And that my mother has had breast cancer.

1990, Texas

The drain tube snakes from under her robe. There is yellow and purple bruising up to her neck. Her breast has been neatly cut away. What was once a breast is now only a hollow slump of chest wall, with skin neatly pulled together and puckered with black wires of stitches.

"Ugly, isn't it?" she says quietly. "Yesterday was the first day I could make myself look at it. But I'm doing okay. I had the best night's sleep the night before the surgery. I could feel everyone praying for me."

"You really slept?" I ask, incredulous.

"Yes, I just have such a feeling of peace about everything."

I kneel at her feet, reapplying the polish the doctors had asked her to remove before surgery. I wonder about the prayers, which must still be floating around her like wishes. When I rub lotion into the balls of her heels, she smiles. Her feet are my feet, with the same two curling toes and high arch. Her hands are my hands. Her face is my face. "My clone," she has always called me.

"This is genetic, you know," she warns softly.

"I know."

"I'm so sorry, Baby."

Now I stand at the high altar of the mammogram machine. How many women supplicate themselves here each year, not daring to breathe? In this state of Texas, 12,300 women are expected to be diagnosed with breast cancer this year, and nearly 2,600 will die. More than 180,000 women in the United States (and 1,000 men) will be diagnosed; 40,600 will die. Worldwide, 1.2 million will die.

The machine only whirs and clicks impassively. It knows nothing of numbers.

To the side of the machine is a Christmas wall decoration of Santa in his sleigh. He holds Rudolph under his right arm, cradled like a small fawn. Rudolph, little mouth open in glee, is looking ahead as they are apparently flying through the sky. It is a strange decoration. Why is Rudolph *in* the sleigh? Santa seems to look right at me. *He sees you when you're sleeping; he knows when you're awake. He knows if you've been bad or good . . .*

Does he know if I have cancer? Old Saint Nick, who was probably a priest and then a bishop around AD 300, is only an extension of a pagan winter gift-giving holiday. He is a mere religious sleight of hand—a shadow god who offers childish delight but no comfort.

The technician steps on a pedal that lowers the plate.

"Ow!" I shout.

She stops humming but says nothing. She offers no apologies. I'm gripped painfully in a vise and then released. And then positioned again. And again. And again. The machine hums and the developer beeps behind me. The tiny veins on my breast are like tributaries of rivers in pale snow.

Six slides of my life will be held up to light.

Santa grins at me with a twinkle in his eye. I am before him bare-breasted, half-naked. Half-wild. The Mayans sacrificed their blood, their animals, their prisoners, even some of their children for the gods. I have seen a child's skull in a cave, killed long ago to be forgotten in a ceremonial pot. The baby's skull had the color and fragility of a sand dollar, unbroken in brown sands of limestone and shadow. Horrible, yes. But when it is your life on the line, or the love for your god, how far would *you* go? Abraham was willing to sacrifice Isaac, his favorite son. What would I be willing to sacrifice now, for my life? A breast? Two?

One in eight women will get breast cancer. Chew on those numbers, Santa.

1997, Mexico

La Gruta del Palmito means "the Cave of the Palmettos." The cave is so vast that I can't see the ceiling or the walls. Ten football fields could fit here; its main room is larger than Carlsbad's, yet wild, with no lights or tourists' trails. After navigating Paso de la Muerte (Passage of Death) by using a hand rope, we have spent nearly an hour working our way down el Desnivel Grande (the Big Drop). Occasionally, we can hear quiet voices or a soft thudding of rock. Words echo in hollow, faraway tones. The helmet lights from the others look very small in the distance—tiny match-glows of movement. They float in the darkness as if on their own, like Saint Elmo's fires. It is hard to remember there are people beneath them.

Reaching bottom in a place called el Catedral, I'm startled when my light shines on color. Blue. Red. Glimmers of pesos. A square picture frame surrounded by unlit candles. Layers of beautiful flowstone have been defaced by Spanish graffiti, and a small wooden shelf holds votives and a ceramic Jesus. There is a small altar in the rock with a picture of the Virgin Mary.

"Unbelievable, huh?" a caver behind me murmurs. "Some of the townspeople climb down here at Easter to light candles and give offerings. Families, grandmothers, everyone. Their shoes and lights aren't so good either."

It's amazing. We are trained for such rigors, yet sweat still stings our eyes like seawater. But why should I be surprised? People make arduous pilgrimages all the time: pilgrimages to the Holy Land, the road to Chimayo in New Mexico, to the cave of Amarnath in India (where 239 devoted died on the mountain from exposure in 1996). People will crawl on their knees for absolution, for health . . . for hope. Most of the sacred places involve caves, and here in Mexico the pre-Hispanic peoples believed rain and cloud gods lived inside the mountains. With the introduction of Catholicism, carved formations representing the old gods were broken and replaced by cave shrines to the Virgin. It's a sleight-of-hand slip of the heart.

The ceramic Jesus gazes above our heads serenely. Mary looks on impassively as the edges of her picture curl and discolor from the dampness of the cave. I shoulder my gear as our group moves deeper into the cave, taking our lights and voices with us one by one, until the two are again left alone in the perfect silence of the cave. Swallowed, bit by bit, by shadows sheltering total darkness.

* * *

The sonogram technician helps me rest on my back in the darkened room. "Did you finish the mammograms?" she asks.

"Yes."

She reads my face. "Not fun, is it? Some Christmas present you get today, huh?" She smiles. "The radiologists have been busy. So many women put off their tests and then try to get in before January, before their insurance deductibles run out."

"They worked me in. I have a lump."

"Mmmm," she says, as she rolls the wand that aims high-frequency sound waves into my breast. "I see it."

I watch the screen as its grainy black-and-white images jerk and pan. "There it is," she points. But I can't make the lump out. The screen is as indecipherable as a black-and-white, upside-down topography map.

It is the cave of my body. The blood that is under her sonogram wand is really rushing through my veins like chaotic, underground rivers through stone. With a resting heart rate, it will circulate completely through my body—from my lungs, to my heart, through my body, and back to my heart again—in only thirty seconds. What wonders are under our skin! I was born with all the eggs I will ever have, thousands of them, and the ability to feed the life that one could produce. Limestone is only slightly harder than my bone. My fingernails are harder than gypsum. The strongest substance in the world could be a woman. We are human, humus, earth—together and one. Our bodies can hold so many secrets inside . . . but secrets that could turn on us on any given day.

2001, Belize

We have come through the cave and up on the other side of the valley ridge. Twilight creeps over the jungle canopy and on the humid air come occasional breezes laden with the fragrance of the blossoming orange groves in the valley. My guide looks down at the trail and stops abruptly. "Up ahead is a little kitty."

Bird calls have gone silent. I see nothing in the brush. But at my feet are fresh tracks of an ocelot—four wild sunbursts with petals of toes.

* * *

A doctor enters the room, introduces himself, and leans over the technician as she keeps the sonogram image steady.

"Here it is," she says to him lowly.

"Hmmm . . . well, it's not a cyst," he says to me. "It's not fluid filled. I can see it's solid. It's something we may need to take out at some point, after we watch it for a while. Your doctor will meet with you next week when she gets the reports back from the mammograms, and she may have some different advice. But I wouldn't worry about it now."

I am wished a Merry Christmas and left alone in the sonogram room to dress. Just like that. To wait and not to worry for a week. Was he too cheerful? Was her smile forced? Am I not to worry because it's nothing, or because it's Christmas?

Lechuguilla. Lech-uh-GEE-ya. I say the word in my mind like a prayer, an incantation. Two of my colleagues should be coming out of this New Mexico cave today from a weeklong expedition, and I long to ask them about it. One can enter this cave by invitation only. Extreme measures are taken to avoid contaminating it. Inside its hundred-mile mazes, explorers cannot comb their hair, disturb the water, move off trail, or leave anything behind, not even hairs or skin cells that float as dust. Why? Among many things, some of the microbes collected from deep in its pristine depths have been shown to "eat" breast cancer cells. Lechuguilla. Our dark hope.

The jaguar god . . . he was the god of life and death.

After all the sacrifices, deaths, prayers, and pilgrimages that have been made in caves, can life emerge now? Has a prayer actually been answered? And will it be in time for me?

1995, Austin

The cave is as small as a hobbit hole. I check it off my survey list of county karst features, and emerge back in the sink area. Here, the ground is sloped to a moist area where green moss clings to the sides of trees. One can hear the slipstreams from a nearby highway, but all noise is muffled. It is strangely quiet. Several large trees encircle this sink area and, like people, seem just as aware of my presence as I am of theirs. They are very old. Their thick bark is black, peeling, and twisting. Their arms are contorted like roots.

Autumn leaves fall from their limbs as if being scattered from arthritic fingers.

I have a feeling of being watched—not malevolent but yet quite distinct. There is no one here now, but neighborhood teenagers have been to this place. Lavender wax from some secret ceremony has run down and pooled in ripples around the base of the trees, like a frozen sea eddy. There are Mountain Dew cans and incense burners. This place is called Witches' Sink. Do the teenagers come to this place because of its presence? Or does the place have a presence because of their pilgrimages?

What could pull them from the modern comforts of satellite TV to come and light candles in silent woods? What shadows still remain in our hearts?

It is still Christmas Eve and the church is full. There are no lights, only candles. Underneath my sweater the technician's ink is still marking a great black X on my breast. I think of woods full of trees doomed to fall from similar painted marks; I look at the lines of women in the church pews and think, "Who next? Which one of us will be cut first?"

My father helps pass the Communion trays through the pews for the Lord's Supper. In the low light the juice in my cup seems to glimmer thickly, just like the blood it is to represent. Although this day was originally decreed in AD 354 as the Roman's feast for Saturn, the Christians made it their own. Tonight is a remembrance of God's sacrifice of a son. Tonight is a remembrance of our own redemption.

My mother, cancer free for over ten years, sits beside me and is as beautiful as the day she showed me her scar. If *I* am to have surgery, would I have the peace to be able to sleep as soundly as she did? I don't think so. Where is my faith like my mother's? Where is my faith like my father's? How does one *feel* a prayer? What is so wrong with me that I have to question that which I shouldn't have to?

Perhaps I have been going to caves for the wrong reasons. Perhaps I should have been lighting candles and incense, drawing blood, beating my chest, and tearing at my hair.

"Some say that the unrolled skin of the jaguar is the night sky and stars."

"They say it's genetic. I'm so sorry, Baby."

"He sees you when you're sleeping; he knows if you're awake . . ."

"Behold, a virgin shall be with child, and shall bring forth a son, and they shall call his name Immanuel, which being interpreted is, God with us."

It's growing cold outside. I hope the black cat that darted in front of me this morning has a home, and will stay warm and safe from the road. I hope that my mother's cancer never comes back. I hope for so many things.

Silent night, holy night. All is calm, all is bright . . . To end the service we sing a cappella, with only our voices breaking the silence of prayers. Then comes that moment—that sweet moment after singing when the sound is still caught up in the rafter beams and reverberates into silence. The after-moment when no one moves; when we are all listening together.

And I know that it will be all right.

The church doors open to the chill night and we emerge. Several women slip their arms around me in an embrace that tells me that they know of my morning pilgrimage today, and are waiting with me. They are strong. Above in the night sky spin Orion, Ursa Major, Cassiopeia, Pegasus, Andromeda. The old gods have not died. They still shadow our lives, listening to the ticking clocks in our breasts. The star that gleamed over a small village in Judea thousands of years ago may have dimmed these spirits, but did not diminish them. For high above our church steeple are all the winter constellations and the jaguar's skin in movement. Fate and hope pad silently along the trail of the Milky Way, tracking and stalking all our days, one by blessed one.

origin moment

SUSAN CERULEAN

It was over South Carolina's Edisto River that I saw my first swallow-tailed kite. My memory is etched with a clear image of how that bird swung into view and hung over me, suspended like an angel, so starkly black and white, with its wide scissored split of a tail. I rushed to grab binoculars, almost flipped the canoe. The bird rode a breeze too subtle to sense, its breast a center point for the sleek maneuver of wing and tail, as if a kite string actually were attached to the deeply muscled breastbone. As suddenly as it appeared, the bird was gone.

Perhaps you have seen these wonderfully adroit flyers, living origami, drifting over a wild southern river, using their deep forked tails as sensitive rudders. Although kites are large—with a wingspread wider than a red-tailed hawk—they are hard to keep in sight, or follow very far. If you have been lucky enough to spot one, you probably hope to repeat the experience.

When that first fleet kite shadow darkened my face, and I lifted my eyes, astonished, to watch the bird wheel above the river's sunny run, I knew that something essential had come into my life connecting me viscerally to wildness. I wanted that wildness. I wanted to leap out of the boat, to scramble over the abrupt knees of the cypress, and climb the insufficient wild aster vines. I wanted to follow that bird.

Only now do I begin to have words for what I felt, half-crouched within the confines of the silver canoe. I begin to name the wild desire that strained my body toward that awesome bird. I can begin to sketch how, in that swamp, my life fully opened to the world of the swallow-tailed kite, an unimagined gift from some god.

To me, kites are about surprise. Mystery. Being gifted. Except when they nest or gather to migrate, it is hard to specifically "bird" for swallow-tails. You can increase your chances of finding them by looking in the right places. It's best to just be in the right places, and let them come to you. In this part of the world that means getting out on the rivers in the summer months. When I drive up the west coast of Florida, north from Tampa to my home in Tallahassee, climbing the ladder of latitude, I slow at each river crossing, and look skyward: Little Waccasassa, Waccasassa, the broad Suwannee, the Steinhatchee, Spring Warrior Creek, the injured Fenholloway, the Econfina, the mysterious Aucilla, the Wacissa, the St. Marks, and dozens of creeks in between. You still can't be sure of seeing a kite, but that's how I increase my chances.

The swallow-tailed kite is a flexible and enterprising bird, and like life itself, intends to inhabit every place she can. A sky-rider, this raptor seems to affect the wetlands and the forests even less than most of the other birds. The emerald marshes never feel the kite's full weight, nor do the great river swamp forests. The bird will cleave the surfaces of our rivers and springs on the wing, to drink or cool its belly, splintering the surface calm for only seconds. When they are here, kites nest high in pines, picking thousands of dragonflies, wasps' nests, anoles, and small snakes from the foliage of the nearby forested wetlands, but neatly with their feet, never stopping their flight. Long stretches of the bird's time on our continent, raising a chick or two, kites go unremarked by human eyes.

Not so long ago, the swallow-tailed kite was able to build her nests as far into the continent's heartland as Minnesota; south and west to Texas; and then northeast to Maine. You might even have seen one in northern New Jersey in a good year—if you had been born before the turn of the twentieth century. Like many creatures, swallow-tailed kites have interacted little with humans, except to respond to our uses of the land. This particular bird's response has been an alarming decline in breeding range and population. Biologists like to draw range maps of the creatures they study, indicating with color bars and dashed lines where the animals nest, migrate, and over-winter. If you compare a present-day range map for the swallow-tailed kite with a presettlement range map for the bird (that is, before the northern European colonizers brought this continent to its knees), the contemporary version looks as if someone had applied heat to a thin film of colored ink, shrinking it into some-thing so small that you want to cup your hand over the page to pro-tect from the frightful, drying air those bits of places where kites still live.

I have never lived outside the kite's dwindled North American home range since I came to Florida thirty-four years ago. At first, of course, I had no idea that I shared their diminished space, nor even that they existed; but maybe, just as we are unconsciously formed by the living spirit of a landscape, we can be drawn to our place and our work, even to something as specific as the breeding range of a bird.

Among the Dagara tribe of West Africa, it is believed that unborn children, approaching their time in the fastness of their mothers' wombs, know their purpose in the world. In a ritual conducted dur-ing the mother's pregnancy, a shaman-priest asks the child-who-is-to-come, "Tell us why you have been sent, your purpose for visiting us." Through the voice of its mother, who is in a trance, the child replies to the shaman and other family members. The grandfather of the child names him or her accordingly, and later acts as confi-dante and guide, helping the young one assume the life program she indicated to her elders while still in utero.

Among my people, the northern Europeans who translocated to the North American continent during the last two hundred years, I have imagined that another way used to be given to the growing child to help her know her path: the tending of her own origin moment.

For us, our human origin moment is the instant when our base-rock, permanent images, and assumptions begin to form as the planet becomes aware of itself through this new being, as it never has before. Wherever a child is located, all that she remembers is her origin moment, and she will live her life forward from this moment of convergence, with whatever emotional overtones and cultural assumptions are included. Among my people, this occasion customarily happens between the ages of one and two years. In other times, the origin moment probably could be traced back much earlier, but our lives have constricted in matters of the old spirit ways.

These origin moments set the course of the lives of the wild animals, as well as ourselves, and it is not so difficult to understand how the wind in the thin tops of tall pine trees informs even the embryos of swallow-tailed kite chicks in the egg, and why they forever return to such fragile circumstances to build their own nests as adults.

In my earliest memory, I stood alone in a crib, my hands gripping a smooth wooden rail, in a warm and darkened house. Outside a window, miles down and away to the southeast, blazed the brilliant electric lights of New York City. Between me and Manhattan Island, where my father went to work each day, I sensed the dark marshlands, the second-growth foothill forests, and the dimmed stars. I fell into my human awareness from this place of watching. Behind me, although I was just barely over a year old, slept my baby sister in a second crib. Beyond her bed was the closed door to my parents' bedroom. At the time memory and spirit recognized one another in the small child of my body, in the early 1950s in northern New Jersey, no swallow-tailed kites were anywhere nearby. It must have been January when I stood in my crib looking to the south and east, and it was dark outside and kites do not often fly after dark, nor in the winter cold. What I knew instead was the frosty outbreath of northern Appalachian trees, the fragrance they exhaled, and the way the snow melts on the south side of those trees and how cold shadows protect the snow on the northern exposure, striping the hillside white longer into spring than seemed bearable, especially for a (once again) pregnant mother of two very young children, such as my own mother. I knew that early winter darkness, and the long spaces of the minutes between the drop of the dark and the hour when my father's train would return him home from New York City.

Without even a word, my mother taught me this about time, how it is elastic, like the potential range map of a bird, and how it can drown you, or bring you quickly to your heart's dearest dreaming.

So I would not have seen the swallow-tailed kite in my earliest years. The spring delivered robins in May (not the winter redbreasts that flock to the native hollies where I live now in northern Florida), but never a kite. Until I was in my early twenties, my experiences of birds were surprised sorts of encounters, chancy moments, unpatterned. In kindergarten, I was taught songs about orioles and robins singing sweetly in spring, but no one knew or could convey the seriousness, nor the dependability, nor the pattern of their return. My family lived season to season, loving the natural world but not fully aware that we were actually of it. We thought of the birds, the seasons, the landscape, all things wild, only as they affected our needs and comforts.

How was it, then, that I came to so love this wild bird, and care for its continuance on our planet?

"I've got a new book to read to you children tonight," my father announced one evening in the winter of my seventh year. "It's about birds. And there's a special part for each of you to do, to help me tell the story. One of you each night." He settled himself comfortably against the headboard of the double bed he shared with my mother. Our family had grown to four children: girl (me), girl, boy, girl.

"Me first, me first," we all hollered, pushing in close, scrapping for his attention and the novelty of the new book.

"Oldest to youngest, this will be Susie's night," my father said firmly. Happily surprised, I scrambled onto his lap, curling my toes into the white chenille bedspread. I crooked an arm around the channel of his neck, feeling privileged, singled out. Usually, the younger two went first. My second sister, Bobbie, quickly claimed our father's left side; the little ones staked out the foot of the bed. Dad tilted the big book so everyone could see, at least sort of, but I got to hold one endleaf of the new treasure myself. Dad opened *Birds of America* to the first page, and began to read aloud an account of a single wild bird, the scarlet tanager. He told about where it lived, the colors of its feathers, how it constructed its nest, how many babies hatched from its nest. I listened, but all the time I was waiting for him to finish, because then I would be allowed to tear a picture sticker of that bird from a sheet of gummed postage stamp images illustrating thirty-six of the kinds of birds appearing in the book. I could see that my youngest sister and brother wouldn't be allowed to do this part; they might rip across a stamp, which would ruin a bird, ruin the new ritual. They had begun to tussle on the end of the bed, already lost from the story.

I stared at the image in my hand. Even flat and so much smaller than life size, the crimson of the bird's body entranced me, and the ebony of its wings and tail.

"Lick the back of it," Dad said. "Stick it anywhere you want, on the scarlet tanager's page."

I touched my tongue to the back side of the stamp, activating the bitter glue, and pressed the picture firm against the page, as straight as I could manage. With my fingernails, I picked at the tiny ragged tears at the stamp's edge so my bird could float perfectly on the creamy white page of Dad's new book.

Perhaps my longing after birds was cemented on the summer deck of the *Miss Ocracoke*, one of the car ferries that transported people and their goods between Hatteras Island and Ocracoke to the south. As my mother steered our family station wagon aboard the ferry, I watched through the open window as laughing gulls and pelicans vied for perches atop the enormous harbor pilings. The ferry attendants moved between the cars, swinging heavy wooden blocks by short rope hanks, shoving them against the cars' front tires to hold them in place for the brief open-water crossing. Then we were allowed to scramble onto the flat gunmetal gray deck. The air was rank with diesel fumes and the clank of chains. We felt the engine's growl through our feet. As the men cast off from the massive shore-side dock and hooked a chain across the ferry's stern, the seagulls lifted from the harbor pilings, collecting around us, dozens and dozens of them, each exactly alike, ebony-capped, screaming.

"Can we have some bread?" we begged our mother, but she waited until the boat entered the main channel, until the winds blew the diesel out and away, and the sharp salt air filled our lungs. Then she divided the bread she had brought into five portions—my share was one and a half slices of the squishy brown stuff (we never threw gulls the good bread, the white Pepperidge Farm sandwich loaf my father preferred). I tore at the crust, peeled it like the skin of an orange. It was too long to give away all at once, so I ripped it into chunks, pushing my wind-whipped hair from my eyes, as the birds circled and shrieked. Then I rolled torn fragments of the bread's interior into doughy balls; these had more weight on the wind, and were easier to aim and toss.

Close, hungry, insistent, bold, brassy, the gulls approached like no other bird we knew. Their black feet dangled just over our heads, and their wings beat high. I tried to direct my bread toward a particular bird, maybe one a bit slower or more timid than the others. I liked to imagine that I was feeding an individual, that my offered food would matter to that bird, that we could be in relationship.

The ultimate achievement in feeding the ferry gulls was to lure one to feed directly from your hand. The birds didn't want to come this close; to take your bread in this way, they had to overcome an innate fear of humans. They had to give up their preferred method of feeding—the airborne snatch with no contact. I slowed myself down into a deep patience, held back somehow, even though all around me my siblings were yelling with delight and abandon, tossing their crumbs to the wind and the birds. I pushed away my own fear—that the bird would take some of my fingertip with the bread—and extended my arm straight out of its socket, long through the elbow, tried to will bread and hand and wrist into one, so that I could win the dare between us. Which of us wanted more fiercely: me, to feed the bird; or the gull to eat my bread?

What I longed for was connection with a single bird, through my physical hand. I wanted to experience the particularity of my gift received, and to believe that I could make a difference in the life of a single bird, even. But the bird, once fed, would wheel away to gobble its prize, and I would lose sight of it in the general feeding frenzy at the ferry's wake.

Perhaps, like me, you have felt at your core some similar, perhaps unnameable longing; a hunger for intimacy (with a person or an animal or a landscape) that does not seem to correspond with the privileges and abundance of your life, and which sometimes drives you to do or consume things you'd rather you hadn't. My journeys after kites have led me to understand that the power of our longings is placing the integrity of life on our tender emerald planet so greatly at risk. We stand, as Thomas Berry tells us, at the end of the Cenozoic age, the great flowering age of plant and animal diversity. Our own species must stare full face at the annihilation we are inflicting. I wonder about the fault lines in our own culture. What are the fractured places in our hearts and minds and spirits that have allowed us to stand by and watch, and even to participate, in the destruction of so much of life? How might we invoke transformative powers, very different from those that seem to rule our world just now?

fire

MATT DALY

In the summer of 1988, the landscape I love caught fire. By the
time October snowstorms brought an end to that long, dry season,
nearly one and a half million acres in the Greater Yellowstone
Ecosystem had burned. Jackson Hole, where I live, was just south of
the largest fires, and we saw pillars of smoke at the edges of the valley. All summer the thunder cracks made me flinch. I feared that the
photographs of Yellowstone in the local newspaper—sepia skies
filled with smoke and endless corridors of blackened trees—could
easily be this valley, these forests, my home. I remember waking
early one morning with fear coiled tight in my belly, convinced the
Tetons above Jackson were burning.

Almost twenty years later, a casual glance reveals little evidence
of the fires of 1988. The ecosystem in this part of the Rockies is well
adapted to fire, and once strong winds blow down the blackened
snags, the shoulders of the mountains can look rich and abundant,
as if never touched by flames.

After being away for a decade, I moved back to my childhood hometown of Jackson Hole with my partner, Cindy, in the late spring of
2000. A year later we would marry under a golden band of autumn
cottonwoods at the edge of the Snake River. Jackson Hole holds most

of my childhood memories, and now it is also the place Cindy and I consider home. Living here, we watch the landscape change through the seasons, year after year. We notice the natural heralds of these changes: the arrival of rough-legged hawks signals the coming of winter, the brilliant flashes of male bluebirds over patches of snow are a sign of spring, and the dust-dry smell of sage tells us the season of summer thunderstorms is here again. The cycle of changes in the Teton country reminds us of our own history, too. The changes in the land remind us of how we have had to change to live together, through times of bounty and through times of crisis.

In August of 1988, a lightning strike at the edge of Shadow Mountain caught in the tinder-dry duff and flames rolled up the slopes on the eastern flank of Jackson Hole. The Hunter fire, as it would be known, immediately threatened the cabins of the Teton Science School and, on my birthday, forced the evacuation of the school's inhabitants. I was driving south out of Yellowstone that day with some friends. The Hunter fire was just one of many fires burning in the Greater Yellowstone Ecosystem, but it was the closest to my home, the most ominous of my life. The air rushing in the open windows parched my throat. At high points along the road out of the park, we could see plumes of smoke billowing up like thunderheads, great columns flattening into tabletops of ash. Driving into Jackson Hole we saw the lone pillar of smoke drifting up into the otherwise blue sky. We watched that steel-gray plume grow broader and more substantial. No one spoke.

By the beginning of the winter of 1988, I felt we had experienced a great tragedy in my home landscape. Fear engulfed my perception of the consequences of those fires. I imagined the lodgepole forests of Yellowstone would remain blackened and lifeless. I thought the shoulder of Shadow Mountain, on the east flank of Jackson Hole, would remain a treeless, blackened scar. I feared I would not feel the same love for the landscape when the snows melted, that I would not recognize my homeland through all the standing black snags. Having no prior experience with such dramatic events, I doubted my own ability to love the place in the aftermath of the fires. That winter, the landscape felt broken to me as the storm winds moaned.

* * *

Cindy and I met in the soft heat of the northern Utah autumn, 1996.
She was sitting near me at an acoustic music festival. Throughout
that day, my friends looked for opportunities for us to meet. They
thought dancing might inspire Cindy and her friends to join us, and
in the crowd we might come together. My friend Robyn and I
danced on the sloping grass song after song. Only months later
would Cindy tell me that she had noticed and had said to herself,
"Someday, I'll have someone to dance with like that." Halfway
through the last song of the encore that evening, I approached
Cindy. I have never had much courage at such times. We may have
stood close for a moment before the song ended, but the moment
was brief and I was nervous. She told me she worked in a local natural food store, and then she walked away.

I spent the next few weeks shopping more than I needed to for
organic produce. Several times I saw Cindy, but didn't have the
nerve to speak to her. When I finally did, she was midway through
her first bite of salad after getting braces. She smiled with strips of
green dangling from her top teeth. "You're just going to have to deal
with this," she said. That was the moment I fell in love. She seemed
so comfortable with herself, challenging me to be the same. She had
been alone for several years and was not looking for a relationship.
My most recent relationship had collapsed under the weight of my
partner's infidelity. Cindy and I took our time, letting our feelings
grow.

In the spring of 1989, just after graduating from high school, I came
to a deeper understanding of the role of fire in my home landscape.
For six weeks, I lived at the Teton Science School and studied the
Hunter fire. I spent most days that summer crouched on the blackened slopes of the mountain and in the Ditch Creek drainage. I
learned that the two major forest communities on Shadow Mountain, quaking aspen and mixed conifer, have adapted to respond
vibrantly to fire.

When wildfire rolls through the underbrush in a stand of
aspens, the trees use their complex root systems to regenerate. After
a disturbance, aspens send the energy stored above ground down
into their roots. This shift triggers the emergence of tiny trees. On

some of our ten-meter study plots, so many new trees were growing that we repeatedly lost count. Hundreds of new sprouts. Looking under a large leaf at a frail new tree, I would often find a smaller one popping up.

In addition to the aspens returning in surprising numbers, my strongest memory in the aspen groves is of the spectacular blooms of *Epilobium angustifolium*, or fireweed. On one occasion, I left my research group to flag the remaining study plots we would visit that day. As lunch approached, I walked back toward the van looking for the group. All around me were the four-foot stalks of fireweed plants with blooms of vibrant pink flowers rising up like candle flames at the top of each plant. I literally stumbled into the circle of students who had sat quietly, waiting for my approach. They knew I would not see them disguised amid such brilliant new growth.

Conifer forests in Jackson Hole adapt much differently to fire. Two of the major species have developed unique strategies for surviving in a landscape with fire. The Douglas fir, *Pseudotsuga menziesii*, takes what I think of as a more defensive approach. These trees have very thick bark that protects their trunks from heat and from flame. Many large Douglas fir trees in Jackson Hole carry the scars of multiple fires in their bark. One particularly large Douglas fir that I visited often on the top of a ridge to the east of Shadow Mountain has at least four such scars on the downhill-facing side of its trunk. Waves of unburned bark grow around a smooth tear of bare wood.

Our region's most common conifer, the lodgepole pine, *Pinus contorta*, has adapted specialized cones to survive wildfire. Although lodgepoles produce cones that open in normal years to release seeds into the duff, the trees also produce cones with a heavy layer of resin sealing the cone shut. These serotinous cones need temperatures as high as 140 degrees to melt the protective coating so the cone can open and the seeds can fall on a forest floor cleared of impediments to the seed's purchase in soil.

After the summer studying Shadow Mountain's response to fire, I cannot walk through the aspen and conifer forests of Jackson Hole without looking for evidence of old fires. Crouching on my hands and knees to watch the forest start over is a memory that will always live deep in my heart.

* * *

In the late winter of my first year with Cindy, our relationship felt
the first cracklings of disturbance. I would wake in the night to the
soft sounds of Cindy crying, or she would wake me and ask me to
hold her. Curled around her, I could feel her heart racing in her
chest. At first, lying like that together would quiet the turmoil and
we would fall back to sleep.

Later nights found us up together, Cindy sobbing and barely able
to breathe. The panic that rose in her did not have one clear cause.
We identified several triggers: the death of Cindy's mother when she
was thirteen, the betrayal that ended a previous love affair, the
stress of a new career. Yet identifying these ignition points could not
stop the full conflagration. Once a panic attack started, it seemed
nothing could hold it back. Panic is unique among anxiety disorders
in that the fear of a panic attack itself becomes the trigger for the
next attack. When Cindy's anxiety was at its height, it too would
contribute to its own spreading. I remember days when I watched
her whole being burst into panic, explode into a column of flame.

In 1988, the conditions in the Greater Yellowstone Ecosystem
were primed for fire. It was not that the land experienced an inordi-
nate number of lightning strikes or abandoned campfires. Rather,
the overall climate was so well suited for extreme fire that it
required only the slightest spark. Once ignited, fire quickly rose up
and created conditions that contributed to its own spreading. Winds
created by the heat of the fire flung out brands miles ahead of the
leading edge. The North Fork fire, which was actively suppressed
from the day it was first identified, still burned a half million acres.

Anxiety and panic disorder affect all aspects of a person. The
emotional and psychological exhaustion made it almost impossible
for Cindy to function normally, even when an attack subsided. One
of her lowest points occurred over the 1996 Christmas holiday season. Cindy returned to Wisconsin to visit her family, and I was on
vacation with my relatives in Mexico. Before the trip we talked about
being apart, about the possible sparks for her anxiety, about her
father and brothers. We tried to think through all of the emotions
that would be in the air that season. But we could not plan for every
possible situation. On her way home, Cindy picked up a flu bug. She
became very sick and vulnerable. Cindy's family, although loving,

faced their own challenges when she fell ill. Years before, Cindy's mother, Joanne, had entered the hospital with pneumonia on Christmas Day. She was deaf and not fully capable of communicating her suffering to her children. She died on January 5, 1983. When Cindy first described that terrible winter, she made it seem to me that Joanne died because she no longer felt the desire for living. As a child, Cindy had seen the depths of her mother's suffering but was too young to help.

Joanne's life and death haunted Cindy and her family when Cindy became ill. As the youngest child and the only girl, Cindy held a special place for her father and two brothers. Through crackling telephone connections, I could hear the fear and exhaustion in Cindy's voice. I could hear the worry of the whole family. My shared worry mixed with a deep feeling of helplessness. Cindy was far away. When we both returned to Salt Lake City, she looked hollow, pale, ravaged, her skin the cold gray of aspen wood stripped of its delicate bark.

Cindy's recovery was slow and marked by unexpected bouts of panic. After acute attacks, we would often spend the day in bed exhausted, crying and resting. For Cindy, panic also brought on nausea, vomiting, and lack of appetite. More than once, we ended up in the emergency room with Cindy severely dehydrated. One night Cindy woke up nauseous after eating at a local diner. She started vomiting. The food poisoning quickly brought on a panic attack and the panic increased her sickness. We huddled on the cold floor of my bathroom while she wept and heaved bile. Her skin was covered in sweat. In the middle of the panic attack Cindy feared she would not survive the night. We rushed to the emergency room. Intravenous fluids helped bring Cindy back from that hopeless moment. After one bag of fluids, she had stopped crying. After two, she could joke about the graveyard shift nurse whose skin was more ashen than hers and whose breath smelled like cigarettes. After the third bag, three liters of fluid, Cindy was finally able to sleep. Watching her sleep in the blue fluorescent light of the windowless room, I felt surrounded by blackness, a charred landscape with no signs of recovery.

We found our way out of that time. Like wildfire, panic attacks pass and may leave behind an altered landscape, open for new growth. Cindy spent hours in therapy and hours more talking me through her discoveries. We talked of Cindy's mother and of her memories of childhood, joyful and terrible. She began to take medication to hold off the worst of the disease. We huddled close together in those days. Cindy was building a thicker skin around her scars. We became closer to our friends and community and stuck close to those people who were most helpful and healing for Cindy. At the same time we learned to celebrate the times when Cindy felt well and happy, and to lie low through the outbursts of the disorder.

A key step in our relationship's recovery from the hardships of panic disorder was our move from Salt Lake City to Jackson Hole. In the landscape of Shadow Mountain and the Tetons, we found healing. A few weeks after our move, it became apparent that time spent out in the wild country surrounding us could help prevent the panic from raging through Cindy. When we saw her anxiety building, we could go for a hike or sit at the edge of one of the lakes at the base of the Tetons and feel the panic subside. For me, walking across a moraine full of young lodgepole pines emerging from serotinous cones served as a reminder that all landscapes hold the capacity to adapt and heal. Our relationship developed deep roots during our struggles. In a healthy landscape those roots could send out new growth.

I planned to ask Cindy to marry me on a trip to Yellowstone in October of 2001. Sometimes seeds take time to germinate. I had the ring tucked safely in my backpack, anticipating finding the perfect spot. The first night of that trip we sat on the shore of Yellowstone Lake at moonrise. The blue-white light of the near-full moon lit the surface of the lake. There was no wind. At the far edge of the lake we could see the outline of the still-standing remnants of the fires of 1988. This was the perfect spot, the perfect moment. But the ring was in my backpack back at the Lake Hotel, a half a mile away.

On the way home from that vacation, I was desperate for another perfect spot to propose. One place by the Snake River was occupied by an elk hunting camp with horse trailers and pickup trucks belching diesel fumes. South of Leigh Lake, another favorite spot was crowded with spectators, looking out across the shimmering surface of Jenny Lake toward the Tetons. All of us were looking for our perfect place. I finally made an excuse to stop at the ranch where I worked at the time. The day was clear. Another of those bright blue days that stand witness over so many of the comings and goings in our valley. We walked to the Snake River over dry cobbles. At the edge of the water, I asked Cindy to marry me, and at that moment a boat full of young fishermen floated past. My back was to them, and when they saw her face red from crying, at first they leaned forward with concern. One man seemed ready to leap from the boat to help her. She raised her arm, fingers blooming upward to show them the ring. They cheered and hooted until passing around the next bend.

In Jackson Hole, each summer we live in anticipation of the fire season and wonder if our favorite forests might burn. We ready ourselves with a mix of fear and excitement. Perhaps a special grove will burn to black. It takes a generation for a charred lodgepole forest to rise up again. Yet in the interim, the blanket of fireweed and other forbs that spring up on the cleared ground, often in the weeks immediately following the blaze, find a rich seedbed amid the first growth of new trees. These new meadows and clearings are usually encircled by groves of trees that avoided the catastrophe. The forests in our valley are richer and more diverse thanks to wildfire.

Cindy's anxiety is manageable now. We know what situations create the conditions for panic to spark in her. We know how to find our way through those moments and to stay vigilant for the possibility of change that follows. There are still times when we fail in our efforts. At these times, I see us taking lessons from our home landscape. We use our past experience to help us see that while an incident might scar us, it does not exhaust the energy of the heart.

We also find opportunities for vibrancy. When the cycle moves far from anxiety and panic, we celebrate and fling ourselves into our community. Cindy loves social interaction, and often after a disturbance she fills the lives of our friends and acquaintances with her most vibrant colors. At these times, my thoughts turn to fireweed and to aspen groves. I feel the abundance returning to Cindy's life, to our life together. Sometimes, the disturbance of anxiety reveals the seeds of what is best in Cindy's heart.

When we move through the moments when panic does burst into our relationship, I think of the trees on Shadow Mountain. I remember that, despite their highly flammable sap so close to the surface, subalpine fir trees still thrive in the shadows of north-facing slopes. I remember the aspen saplings, now much taller than I am, and the stalks of fireweed. I think of the lodgepole pines and wonder what new seeds will be revealed by fire in our lives and how to best nurture them when they fall.

Into this complex landscape, Cindy and I are now raising our child. We both look forward to taking him to visit the places we love. We will go to Yellowstone, to Leigh Lake, and to Shadow Mountain. I will bend down with him in the blackened earth and ash to search for seedlings. Perhaps we will carry a little spring water, cupped in our hands, to wet the new growth. I have now spent more than half my life in Jackson Hole. With each season I feel more strongly that my relationship to this place is as close to any I have with a person. From that awareness I take comfort and some knowledge of how to carry forward in my life with Cindy and our son. I see the land we live in as our closest advisor in matters of the heart.

leaving vinland

DIANE HUETER WARNER

I caught only fleeting glimpses of eastern Kansas, with its rolling hills, pastures, oak forests, and stone walls, as our station wagon skimmed down dusky country roads. With this station wagon full of our belongings, my husband and I had traveled for months, camping out mostly. Leaving Seattle in a February rainstorm, we'd driven down the Pacific coast, over the Golden Gate Bridge, across the Mojave Desert, over the Rockies, and finally through the long flat prairie east of Denver. On this day in May, we'd started early from Salina, where we'd stayed with one of my husband's high school friends, and now we were trying to find other friends of friends, some place in Lawrence where we could spend the night. We drove from farmland to city limits, down the town's main supermarket-movie theater four-laner, to a quiet, tree-lined street of small snug houses with porches lit by parlor windows and fireflies in the bushes and lawns.

That first night in Lawrence, I heard someone say, "We're under a tornado watch." I'd never heard this before and I asked what it meant. "Conditions are right for tornado formation," they said. "We *watch* the clouds and sky. If a warning is issued, it means a tornado has been spotted. Then we take cover." Since this conversation occurred in the black of night, with the rain pelting down and the

howling wind seemingly bent on shoving the low bungalow from its
very foundation, their explanation offered me no comfort, only anxiety and confusion. Then these friendly strangers, teasing the new-
comer, asked, "Remember Dorothy? Remember the Wizard of Oz?"
Oh yes, oh yes, I thought, *this is the land of black and white.*
Everyone slept that night, no one keeping tornado vigil. Even I
slept, exhausted from travel. Morning dawned with only wet lawns
and streets littered with small branches, delicate tree leaves, and
glittering gutter garbage. In the bright morning sunlight everything
sparkled like emeralds.

In Seattle, I was raised with a different model for disaster: the shaking and rolling of the ground. Earthquakes could destroy entire
cities, crumble buildings, split roads, raise tsunamis. You didn't wait
for them, you didn't watch for them. Earthquakes happened unexpectedly while you were doing something else. Years could go by
with no temblors, and you could almost imagine that the earth had
achieved an eternal stability. Yet I remember being ordered under
my school desk one spring day, when the ground, the linoleum
floor, rolled and heaved. It felt as if I were floating in Lake Washington, bobbing on the dissipating wake of a power boat far out in the
water. The hanging fluorescent lights above us swayed on their
chains, the pine trees outside the windows swayed like dry weeds. It
was not wind that moved them, but a force deeper than their roots. I
think there was a sound, at least in my memory there is a sound,
something between a rumble and a swoosh. When I got home from
school, all my brothers and sisters and I had stories to tell. Our
mother told how the water from our in-ground swimming pool
spilled over the pool's rim and down the steps to the patio and how
all the dishes in the cupboards rattled and she could see the glass in
the picture windows shimmer and waver. That moment she was
afraid, at home by herself, with her six children attending two different schools and Daddy somewhere in downtown Seattle, perhaps
at that very dangerous moment repairing an elevator in the Smith
Tower or the Space Needle. But it was exciting to us, as children, not
scary. Our home stood, our family stood. We fell asleep that night
with no more cares than any other day.

* * *

The first summer in Lawrence, the summer our daughter Josie was born, we lived on the fourth floor of a large concrete structure built onto the side of a hill—Ujama West, a fraternity house then occupied as an experiment in communal living. There was no basement, each floor had its own dormitory-style shower and bathroom, and each room had built-in bureaus and desks, flimsy closets of plywood. Ours was the only occupied room at the end of the hall, next to the exterior stairs. Sometimes I would sit on the stair landing, in leafy shade, drying my hair in the breeze.

The building's best feature in our eyes was the rooftop terrace with sweeping views of the Kaw River Valley. Trees surrounded it and screened the nearest streets and houses from sight; it was like a tree house where I read the poets of my birthplace—Roethke, Niatum, and Stafford—and wrote journal entries and poems. I stood there many times that summer, through my transition from pregnancy to mother with baby cradled in my arms, watching thunderstorms roll in from the west. My husband pointed out the torrential rain that divided the horizon into dark and light halves, while the clouds mounted up higher and higher into the sky, and the lightning flashed when it was too far away to even hear. The freshening breeze from distant storms would lift strands of hair from our sweaty foreheads and necks. Even the rain, I marveled, was a powerful force, completely different from the drizzle and mist of Seattle.

I would write home and tell my mother about my new experiences; and through her, the rest of the family. I would send photographs of this new granddaughter and me on the commune rooftop with the wide expanse of blue sky behind us, and I never wondered if my mother marveled when she saw us because I knew she did.

Year after year, I listened with awkward attention to friends who told me that as children on the farm or in some small western Kansas town, they watched tornadoes from their dinner tables, eating macaroni and cheese, fried chicken, green beans, peach cobbler. Well, tornadoes happen, they seemed to say. In this time of the year, when the temperature and humidity are like this, tornadoes happen; not always, but sometimes. We could see tornadoes coming, they

said, across the flat fields of corn and wheat. And if our father or
mother thought "this is the time," we went to the shelter, full with
dinner, excited and scared, but it was somehow normal, a regular
occurrence. And most of the time, the storm passed without
extraordinary damage or death. These friends didn't seem prone to
superstition, tossing salt over their shoulders to ward off evil,
crossing the street when a black cat strolled down the sidewalk. Nor
did they seem to be adrenaline addicts, looking for the next fix of
speed or danger. They loved, they raised families, they worked and
studied at the university, and they accepted the clouds and the storm
fronts as the backdrop to all they accomplished, all they possessed.

When our daughter Josie was just one year old, and the communal
living experience was waning, my husband and I saw an ad for a
house to rent. What in those few brief words, all newspaper-inky,
attracted us the most? In the country? Woodburning stoves? Outhouse? (Was that even mentioned?) Seventy-five dollars a month
rent? Late August, we went to look at it, getting directions from
Vaughn and Rosie, the owners, who were moving to a family farm
near Manhattan. We drove south out of Lawrence, past the wetlands,
over the Wakarusa River, around and up the hill past the Cedar Hill
Gun Club, and finally turned off onto a dusty gravel road. It was a
twenty-minute drive we were to make twice a day, weekdays only,
for the next ten years.

We stopped in front of a row of Chinese elms, feathery and
graceful. A simple two-story farmhouse, door solidly centered, a tall
window to each side, spirea and Virginian creeper framing the front
porch, the creeper already beginning to turn red. The yard was surrounded by a simple wire fence. A corner of the front porch rested
on cinder blocks, though our tour of the inside convinced us that
the original structure was solid enough. The kitchen was in the rick-
ety add-on—slanted walls, sloping floors, low ceilings—but it had an
electric stove for cooking, a refrigerator, a sink that drained into a
bucket. A pump stood outside the kitchen door and across from it a
root cellar, overgrown with bushes and weeds. There were two out-
buildings, a clothesline under mulberry trees, and . . . the outhouse.
Across the back alley we saw a pasture with grazing cows and calves.

Vaughn and Rosie would leave the woodstoves and the upright piano—which I tested, running my fingers up and down some simple scales. We could have it all, month-to-month, for as long as we wanted.

Cash-strapped and minimally employed, our impulsive natures told us we would be happy in that house; it would be home. Even the village name, Vinland, seemed to regale us with songs of vines, warm evenings, and the bounty of the earth.

Absent from most modern maps, too small for notice, Vinland was a small cluster of buildings. There were two churches (one shuttered with weathered, graying boards; one painted crisply white and holding weekly services marked by bell ringing and a parking area full of station wagons); the Grange Hall (with monthly meetings); a Mercantile (converted to an artist's studio); four small houses, three (including ours) with outhouses; a prosperous dairy farm; and the oldest circulating library in the state, a small red building that lent both Dr. Seuss and Shakespeare. In the heyday of railroad transportation, Vinland had been a thriving community. Later one family turned the long stretch of flat track area into a runway for small private planes and crop dusters. The person closest in age to my husband and me was probably the dairy farmer's ten-year-old son. The community was friendly enough, but we all kept to ourselves. As our widowed neighbor Mae said once, her business was south of the fence line, implying that since we lived north, what we did in our side of the world was not her concern, though she was well aware of it all.

Denise Levertov wrote: "What wild dawns there were / in our first years here / when we would run outdoors naked / to pee in the long grass behind the house." I read these lines so often, from her book *Relearning the Alphabet*, and even now they bring to mind our years in Vinland, and I smile: Who needs indoor plumbing if you can see the Milky Way? Who needs central heat when the woodstove keeps your toes toasty and your drink hot, when it crackles and pops in companionable conversation?

In Vinland, we found hop vines and wild grapes. We grew tomatoes, okra, carrots, and corn. Each year Donn built a stack of firewood by the fence. Cardinals flew to the juniper trees. Coyotes howled on the hills at midnight or trotted down the runway in the dewy mornings. We had snakes in the henhouse, hummingbirds trapped in the wolf spider webs. We had red poppies on the fence line and lightning bugs all summer. Yes, we lost a pup to coyotes. Yes, we found gnawed cattle carcasses when we walked through the snowy fields. One summer we even heard the sound baby rabbits make when they are snatched from their dens.

In Vinland, I wrote poems, baked bread, gave birth to my second daughter one warm December afternoon in the unheated bedroom. It was the time and place where I changed the most. My imagination was seized by the differences in landscapes, and my poems began to explore the history, climate, animals, and plants of the new area. I wrote about my family, both the two-child, one-husband small circle and the larger, distant web of everyone back home, in Seattle. I read new poets: Contoski, Kooser, Elliott, Kloefkorn. I came to know that Stafford, my poet of "Traveling Through the Dark," had a Midwest connection, too. My daughters would pound their chubby fists on the bedroom door, but I would bend myself to my notebook and their father would take them to the pond to catch tadpoles in the squishy mud.

Still, amid the glory of our days, tornado watches could not be dismissed. The one thing I could not accustom myself to, the one thing I could accept with stoicism but not with joy. Tornado watch, tornado warning. I puzzled out the little icons in the corner of our small black-and-white TV. The outline of a swirling funnel cloud meant "tornado watch." Get ready, stay alert. Yes, watch the sky. A solid funnel cloud was a warning. Lives depended on quick and focused action. Take cover, immediately. Basements or tornado shelters were best, but bathtubs or showers and even hall closets could be resorted to in these perilous situations. Pull a mattress in on top; save yourself, save your children.

This still seemed so strange to me, so nerve wracking and stomach churning. I could never get settled. "Will the weather change if I *watch* it?" I asked. How can I protect my family in the black of night? The coyotes sing sweet songs, the fireflies embroider the dark outline of the trees. I accept shivering in winter, I accept burning in summer. I accept chigger bites, mice turds, having to boil water for a bath or to wash my hair. But tornadoes in the stormy night? No fair, God, no fair.

From the porch, sturdy but always a bit lopsided because of the one corner supported by cinder blocks, we had a view as expansive and magnificent in its way as the view from the fraternity house roof. We could see across the airplane runway, across the field of wheat, and the highway, and then in the far distance the ground rising up slowly as if to meet the single tree on the horizon. I usually sat reading, watching Josie playing on the swing set, with Donn sitting beside me or changing the record on the record player. The sun would set in a rosy glow, the fireflies would appear in the lacy leaves of the poppies. But that day, I came downstairs from where I was watching TV while nursing our youngest daughter. Though the day was still hot and humid, and the air was quiet, the icon on the screen was a solid funnel cloud and the name of the county was ours. From the porch, I saw a new object on the horizon, a twisting rope of wind. My eyes registered that it was getting larger, though it appeared to be stationary.

If it looks like it is standing still, but getting bigger, then it is coming straight at you. At that moment my body felt only fear, gut crumbling fear. I balanced Erin on my hip. Barely six months old, she had fuzzy blond hair, blue eyes. She wore only a cloth diaper, her stomach was damp with both sweat and drool. My only thought to alert the others, my husband and Josie, all that mattered. We had to take cover. I felt the hairs and muscles all along my spine tingle and clench with anxiety. I was frozen for a moment, like a dove eyeing the hawk in the air, like a rabbit in a lair. I called for Donn and Josie, and from the front porch we watched, almost hypnotized, as another tornado ripped apart a row of trees bordering a local farmer's field. Donn and I had to be the parents who said it was time to take shelter. This danger was real.

The dirt-mounded root cellar was overgrown with orange trumpet creeper and green flowerless forsythia. It was like a cave and we could see the sky through the holes in the roof. Still, we all took refuge in the crumbling cellar with its ancient collection of canning jars, fruits and beans, and a board bench. We heard thunder and the plunk, plunk, plunk of hail on the cellar's tin-covered door. Donn kept jumping out to take photographs, but the girls and I stayed inside until he gave the all clear. When we emerged from that cave, the sky above our house was blue and clear, though leaves from the Chinese elm and the silver maple littered the yard. Josie picked up flattened pieces of hail from the lawn as if gathering Easter eggs. It seemed so quiet, with just a hint of a sigh, as if everyone and everything needed just to take a deep breath. We were safe, our house stood undamaged, the tornado's force had missed us. In the back, across our neighbor's cow pasture, we could see three tornadoes, far away, like black ropes writhing and then finally pulling the threads of themselves back into the black cloud tapestry.

Our neighbor Mae was surprised the first October we brought Josie down to trick-or-treat. She hadn't made note of the date and she couldn't remember the last time she had had costumed children on her doorstep. Her house was so tiny I could touch the ceiling; it had no indoor plumbing, though it was heated by electric baseboards. Located at the end of our gravel road within fifty feet of a long aluminum airplane hangar, it was tiny, squat, and unpainted. Inside her home, Mae crocheted afghans and pieced together quilts. Mae was fiercely independent and barely sociable to Donn and me, but as soon as Josie could walk and talk, she was determined to be Mae's visitor. Mae gave her cookies and crocheted a pink and yellow baby blanket for Josie's doll. What they did together, I can only guess, but I've never spent a moment worrying about it. I wrote a poem about Mae shaking a pillowcase beneath a mulberry tree, trying to shoo the grackles away. She kept a mean dog on a chain tied to a cement block, the chain just long enough so the dog could protect her front door from unwelcome visitors. Not that anyone ever came to our small community. But then Mae fell down, broke her hip, and was moved to a nursing home, where she died. Her relatives rented her house out to new people. Well, who would buy it?

We were having dinner with Brian and Kaylyn on the picnic table in the cottonwood shade of our front yard. It was a farewell dinner because Donn and I and the girls were soon to be moving back to Washington. Not to lush and rainy Seattle, but to Pullman, nestled in the extreme southeast corner of the state, where Donn had been accepted to graduate school. Brian and Kaylyn had been living in the Mercantile for a few years and were going to rent our house, which we had finally purchased and remodeled so it had both a kitchen and bathroom. We told them we thought we would like to return to Vinland someday, for good friends and slow balmy evenings like this one.

Suddenly, as we sat over the last glass of wine, with the sun still hanging high in the midsummer sky, we sensed a change in the climate. Something was going on down at Mae's house. Propelled by a force we couldn't see, tables, chairs, lamps, boots flew into Mae's front yard. Someone was cleaning house. Someone was yelling. Someone drove away very quickly in a rattling car, raising a plume of dust. Just as suddenly as it had erupted, the air became quiet and calm. We laughed a bit uneasily, cleaned the dishes from the picnic table, said good-night.

Summer nights in Kansas are dark and humid. The warm moist air comes all the way from the Gulf of Mexico in an unbroken sweep across the plains. We sleep with flimsy nightwear, silky, synthetic. We sleep with only a cotton sheet, windows open, cicadas buzzing, trees sighing, trucks straining up Palmyra Hill. On summer nights like this, it takes a while to fall asleep, tossing and sweating and listening. But I am deep asleep, with my husband beside me and our two small daughters in their room across the hall. I wake abruptly to pounding on the door, someone pounding and yelling for help. I grab my robe, hurry down the stairs, open the door—it was never locked, but who would know? And the woman, wild-eyed, plump, short. I cannot read her emotions, in shock myself, the peaceful and secure sleep I fell into every night rent open as if by lightning, the quiet night broken by her distress. I recognize her as half of the new couple in the last house down the road, Mae's house, the house with a front yard littered with boots, broken dishes, furniture, and clothes. She wants to use the telephone. *He ripped the phone out of the wall*, she wails. *The bastard had a gun*, she cries. *He threatened to shoot me. I need to call for help.* I show her the phone, my husband and children still asleep.

But she doesn't call for help, not as I imagine help, immediate authoritative law enforcement. She calls some family member, and curses them roundly. *Get over here*, she shrieks into the phone, standing in my front room, spitting into my night air, cracking my dreams. *Get yer ass over here and take care of him!* Then she leaves, she doesn't even want to wait for her *help* to arrive, but I don't want her in my home anymore. I can't imagine anyone living close enough to our isolated community to be there quickly, and I worry about her, but before I go back upstairs I lock the front and back doors. I stare into the dark night for a long time, puzzled and uneasy. For days, maybe weeks, I wake in the middle of the night, my heart pounding like a fist beating on the door. I can only calm myself with great effort, remind myself that this is leftover terror, as if I had been infected by my neighbor's distress—but how strangely it colors my small world. The place I felt was bounded by Chinese elms, wire fences, and lightning bugs in the tall grass, the place where I had given birth to one of my two children, where Donn and I had taught them both to talk, to count, to make bread and cookies, this place, the place I knew I was leaving, the home of my happiness and hope, no longer felt safe. The thing I had feared, a tornado in the black of night, was not the fiercest thing I or my family could ever encounter.

We moved to Pullman, then Peoria, then Lubbock. We lived on Military Hill, Winnebago Lane, 15th and Slide. A few weeks after we drove a rented van into Pullman, we awoke early one morning to the rolling of the floors and the rattle of plates on the shelves. One fall, I cringed each time I drove to work, as my car wheels passed over the red stain I knew to be a murder victim's blood. In Peoria, summer skies flashed with lightning and pelted hail, and the fierce wind uprooted trees; our neighbor's son shot BBs at our cats. I've been in Lubbock long enough to see flooded streets, walls of red dust, trees split by lightning; the bad things that happen in any city happen here, and the good. In my closet here in Texas, I have many photo albums. Josie lives in Seattle, Erin in Brooklyn, but I have two photos from that last summer in Vinland, perhaps even from the afternoon of our farewell dinner with Brian and Kaylyn. In my mind, without opening the closet door, without taking down one album after another, without flipping page after page, I clearly see my girls. Josie was ten and quietly, joyously serious; Erin was a grinning, charming, and rambunctious five-year-old. We had photographed each of them in turn, securely balanced on Brian's motorcycle that he parked by our front gate. Their hands are covered by black leather gloves and their small faces framed by his helmet's open visor. They bend over the handlebars as if they roared down a long road. I can't tell you everything that has happened since that time, but I know now those images show us leaving Vinland.

angler girl

SUSAN LEIGH TOMLINSON

1. ELK HAIR CADDIS

My father was a fisherman, nearly a century ago when he was growing up on a farm alongside the rolling creeks of northern Alabama. I know this because I've seen photos of him, impossibly young and handsome in a cocky panama hat, proudly holding stringers of silvery fish. Now he's old and bent like a hook so that he stares at the floor all the time. And he's lived for many years in a landscape with no water, no place where fish might lie in wait for his tricks. So he is done with fishing.

I've seen this place where my father was a boy, most recently when I took him back there for the funeral of his older brother, the man who raised him. After the service I rode around in the countryside with cousins I hardly knew, staring hard at all the water we drove across. I tried to imagine him fishing those clear creeks, but it was like trying to put a mental picture to a foreign tongue.

2. ROYAL WULFF

In the evening I drive to the student recreation center for my lesson. We meet on the west side, on the grass next to the basketball courts, where the occasional referee's whistle can be heard over the hard chuff of the wind. A front is moving in and a tall bank of nickel-colored clouds sits on the horizon beyond the arena parking lot. From a distance like this I can imagine that they are mountains and that instead of being here on an irrigated lawn, next to a parking lot full of pickup trucks, I am back in the Hondo Valley.

I'm piecing my rod together when Scott, the instructor of the fly-fishing class, asks if I've had a chance to try any of the flies he picked out for me at the store. There are no streams here and so for a moment I'm confused, but then I realize what he means.

"No," I say.

"You should try it," he says. "They stock trout in some of them."

I must look skeptical, because he says, "No, really. We go to that one at 82nd and Quaker. Well, actually, it's not quite on 82nd. There're some buildings there, a bank or something, and it's behind that. Do you know where I mean?"

I nod, "Yeah, yeah. I know the one."

And he says, "But there're no trout in that one. I don't know which ones have the trout." He's piecing together a rod, too, as he talks. Scott is young and sweetly earnest. I picture the city playas—shallow depressions of pustulant street runoff—and try not to show my opinion of pulling a fish from one of them. Absently, I loop the fly line and the tippet, with its tiny fluff of moon-yellow yarn, through the guides.

Scott has placed three Hula-hoops on the grass. I choose the purple one in the center and circle around it to get the best play of the wind, which is acting variable and tricky—now from the south, now from the northeast, back again. For a moment Scott devotes all of his attention to my casts, remarking on how good they look. And my yarn fly does seem to be hitting the grassy circle inside the hoop with increasing regularity in spite of the changing wind.

Scott now starts to cast into the same spot as he talks. I watch to see how he does it and notice that he doesn't make a prolonged presentation of false casts—the repetitive, preparatory motions that are in every way just like the cast that will put the fly on the water, except that you don't, and the purpose of which is to generate energy and distance, or something like that—he doesn't do this as those of us taking the class normally do. Instead, he whips the line casually:

one, two, then lays the fly in the hoop. It settles there as softly as if he'd cradled it through the air on a thought. I stop my convoluted windups and try the same, and instantly my yellow bit of fluff starts hitting the target on every cast. I decide I'm done with false casting forever.

3. ROGUE FOAM GIANT STONE

Others begin to arrive and start casting into the hoops. We don't talk. Most of the students in the fly-fishing class are also students at the university. I am the outsider here—twice their ages, with a frumpy, unhip air that reveals me to be a professor. Worse, early on in the lessons I gave myself away as someone who knows next to nothing about fishing. On the first evening we were instructed to go around the room and tell everyone else why we were taking the class. Most of the reasons were variations on the same themes:

"I've been a bait fisherman all my life. I want to try something new."

"I caught a trout up around Possum Kingdom. I want to go back to catch some more."

"I want to learn to fly fish so I can fish in Montana."

"—New Mexico."

"—Wyoming."

Then it was my turn. I said, "It's a reason to stand in a stream."

4. BLUE WING OLIVE PARACHUTE

I had to miss half of the first lesson and all of the second for work. At the beginning of the third, Scott watched me cast for a minute or two and said to the rest of the class, "If you want to see a beautiful back cast, you should stop and watch her."

Now, on the evening of the final lesson, everyone studiously avoids looking at me, this non-fisherman, this odd middle-aged woman with the beautiful back cast. I think about this uncomfortable singling out of my skill and my yarn starts going astray, refusing to land anywhere near the hoop. The line whips out in front of me, singing with precision through the air until it reaches a point just above the circle, when it suddenly and mysteriously rips sideways at a hard right angle, and then drops straight down as if shot dead from the sky. Everything begins to go wrong then. The little yarn fly is all over the place no matter what I try—no false casting, many false casts, short back cast, long—it doesn't matter. The line even starts tangling up on itself, and I have to pause often to work on the snarls. And worst of all, my fly is snapping off the tippet on every other back cast. My beautiful back cast, of which Scott was once so proud.

I pause to tie the fly back onto the leader using a surgeon's knot, which I've read about in a book. Since I've missed so many of the classes, I've been secretly supplementing Scott's instruction with literature on the fine art of angling. These books I've collected offer guidance to the reader with a gentle reverence toward this occupation of fish-catching. On the basis of what I have learned from this extracurricular reading, I've also been walking down the street from my house to a small park—a dry playa kept golf course green by irrigation with city water—to practice casting by mimicking what I've seen in the books' photographs. In the hollow of this strangely green playa, I stand like a stick and metronomically sling a fly line back and forth, usually picking out some darker stain of grass for a target. This furry phthalo-green patch is, in my mind, a hole behind a boulder in a stream, where trout lie in wait out of the rush of water. I have read in "the Literature" that this is a good place to spot my imitation fly, which I plan to trick the trout into believing is real by allowing it to float past on the surface, following the current. Apparently this sort of thing happens all the time in nature, and it is more than a fish can bear.

I cast my bit of yarn at the grassy stain and imagine it landing in a stream. Sometimes when I do this it is late in the day, as it is now, and the slanting sun sends a ripple of amber across the playa. Strings of yammering geese fly overhead, returning from a day of feeding in the alfalfa fields. The sun strikes their bellies, lighting them up, and they are suddenly a ragged zipper, piecing together the wide prairie sky. Then the wind flowing over these dry plains makes a hushed sound, and for a moment, I can believe I hear water.

5. DAVE'S HOPPER

I've been trying to remember the first time I ever saw a running stream. Was it in the Hondo Valley, on a Sunday afternoon? My parents—who both grew up in a different, greener landscape and were often lonely for it—sometimes drove us there after church to spend the afternoon in the New Mexico mountains. Maybe it was an autumn day, when the aspen were turning and the air hummed with sunlight. In my mind I am remembering a day in which I see roadside fruit stands selling apple cider, and stone spring houses, and horses feeding beneath the tall trees. I see also, woven into the dun-colored grasses of the stream valley, a shimmer of light that is water.

Later that day we stop at a diner in a small town. At the cash register there are boxes with clear plastic lids, and inside are curious beans that hop around under their own power. They are Mexican jumping beans—from a bush in Mexico called, improbably, the jumping bean shrub—and I know now that they're not beans at all, but parts of seeds, and contained within each is the restless larva of a moth. On that day, though, the day that I'm remembering, I'm very young and there's no logical explanation for all this hopping about, and so they are pure magic.

6. DAHLBERG DIVER

Later in the evening, when it is too dark to see where our yarns are landing, we will go inside where Scott shows us examples of famous flies: Royal Wulff, Dahlberg Diver, Elk Hair Caddis, Dave's Hopper. I have seen them all before, though, in the books and catalogs I pore over at night, and know what fish and conditions each is used for. So I'll be daydreaming when a fly comes my way that I do not know. Scott calls it a Clouser, and it is supposed to resemble a minnow.

It's ugly, with long feathers the color of bile, silver bead bug eyes, and a hook big enough to reel in a carburetor. I'll hold it in my hand and feel an odd stirring, like beetles crawling around my heart. It looks like radiation, like pesticide, like fecal coliform. And I know immediately what this poison fly is. This is a playa fly.

The tiny, delicate flies such as might attract trout—flies as airy and full of light as the inflorescence of prairie grass—have been impossible abstractions because they belong to streams; the thought of laying one on the surface of a playa has felt vaguely dissonant and morally suspect to me. The Clouser, however, with its hallucinogenic color and industrial strength hook, seems just the ticket for a toxic pond. Clearly, I have been looking at fishing the playas in the wrong way. I've been looking at fishing them through the lens of beauty, when all along I should have been viewing my endeavors through the more . . . Felliniesque qualities of the playas.

"*Yes, yes, I see now!*" I'll think in a moment of delirium. "*Fish the playas* because *they are strange and un-stream-like.*" I will be filled with hope at this new way of thinking about the playas.

Tomorrow I'll go to Wal-Mart and buy a fishing license. I'll pay $4.95 for this bilious Clouser that has changed my mind about fishing in playas. I'll tie the Clouser onto my leader and cautiously wind my way down to the murky water through the countless noodles of dried Canada goose turds that litter the banks. I'll studiously false cast to get my rhythm down: forward to nine o'clock, back to twelve, letting the rod tip continue to one, punch forward to eleven; repeat. My tippet will snap on a back cast and I'll lose this expensive fly to this nightmare of a prairie lake on my fourth false cast, before ever laying it on the surface of the water.

Later, I'll find the Clouser mysteriously lying at my feet on the dusty water's edge. Scott is right. It looks like a dead minnow.

7. ADAMS

I notice that as I cast I am starting to have a single thought that repeats itself, like a mantra:

It is a reason to stand in a stream.
It is a reason to stand
in a stream.

8. FLASHABOU BEADHEAD OLIVE WOOLLY BUGGER

The literature suggests dividing a stream into imaginary grids, so that as one is standing hip deep in the roiling flow, one might work a section of it more methodically, thereby increasing the opportunity to catch the wily trout. In the book that suggests this, there is a photograph of the author doing just that and looking very sharp about it. It is later in the week and I think on this advice as I cast my line at the playa not quite on 82nd. I've replaced the Clouser with a fly called a Woolly Bugger, thinking that it might be attractive to bass, the most likely fish to be stocked in this stew. Actually, if I were to go on empirical evidence, the *most* likely fish to be here are carp of the overgrown goldfish variety, given that it is their mummified bodies I often see littering the salt flats whenever evaporation reduces the playas to crusty puddles. I am terrified of catching one of these, which are surely former pets set free by young children. Still, which is the least of these for the fish: death by hook, or by drought?

I picture the grid, a largish black net stretched across the surface of the water. Confined within each square of this net, according to the Literature, are possibilities, awaiting my instruction. I squint at the imaginary squares, making sure that these possibilities are not goldfish. Seeing none, I begin my cast.

I'm here by myself on a windy autumn day, picturing a grid that is not there, casting into a soupy lake that is not a lake, hoping I will not accidentally catch a fish that is really a pet. I am here to repair this hole in my heart that is water.

9. MARABOU MUDDLER

It is earlier in the week. We're nearing the end of the semester and the part of the interdisciplinary science class that I help teach in which we talk about the environmental issues of the region. It has been a challenge this fall term getting them to care, even though I spend much of the time extolling the virtues of the prairie. Mostly when I gaze across the classroom at their faces I see a look that says: why am I here? All they know of this place is the cotton-fucked ugliness of the plains; they see it as a burden and punishment to be here. For a moment I think I might try one more time to change their minds. I'm standing at the window and staring down at the courtyard, where freeze-withered ornamental kale and pansies are planted, and I think that I could tell them about the color of late afternoon light, or the softness of tall grasses when you draw your hands through them, or the way the wind can sound like water. But I don't. The prairie is gone, plowed up, sucked dry, and blown away, and I have no answer that they would understand. Instead, I turn from the window and continue my lecture.

"There is no water," I say.

10. CHARTREUSE CLOUSER MINNOW

On the evening of the last lesson, in the minutes before I've seen the Clouser for the first time, the front has arrived with force and the temperature is falling rapidly. My fingers are stiff with cold and I figure I have one more cast in me before I can't feel my hands any longer. All I'm thinking about right now is that this is the last lesson and my experience with the reverent art of presenting a fly to a stream may never get any more real than a bit of yarn and a purple Hula-hoop. It makes hitting the target perfectly a final time tonight both critical and meaningless.

I sling the fly out into the drifting autumn wind, watching as the line unfolds on the sunset in front of me—a tender curl of light, a streak of uncommon grace. The yarn floats softly to the ground, falling toward the center of the hoop, and I think, *"This is it, this is right."* It's nothing more than a fluff of yellow falling into a space defined by a child's toy, but in this perfect instant it is a lit-up zipper of geese in the prairie sky and the hush of wind across the land. It is cocky young men with their proud stringers of silvery fish and the toxic playa Clouser I have yet to see. It is a beautiful back cast by a middle-aged woman. It is a shimmer of light through dun-colored grasses. It is the answer to the question, the reason we are here. Then the wind shifts suddenly at the end and the yarn hops like a curious bean, up and out of the circle.

a day in the park

JORDAN FISHER SMITH

It was midsummer, a couple of years into my time in the
foothills. A white haze filled the canyon of the North Fork of the
American River, flattening its depth and dimensions. The afternoon
heat was somnolent, the still air scented with the volatile spice of
the brush fields.

The sides of the canyon were almost too steep to walk on and
covered in thick stands of live oak, bay laurel, buckeye, and brush,
the average color of which was gray green. A sparse overstory of
ghostly foothill pines cast patches of partial shade, their scabby gray
trunks standing out from the canyon walls at precarious angles. At
the bottom of the canyon a ribbon of blue water made its way southwest, bending back and forth across a broad gray bed of cobbles and
sand. Half a mile downstream it entered a small, narrow reservoir,
which followed the bends in the canyon for a couple more miles to
where it spilled uselessly over a small dam. In the other direction,
white anvilheads of cloud climbed over the high country, thirty
miles east. There was a faint rumble of thunder. A few turkey vultures floated in intersecting circles along the canyon rim, savoring
the hot air for the inevitable attrition of heat, drought, and violence.

A narrow dirt road descended the eastern wall of the canyon, winding in and out of the tributary ridges and gullies. Down it, a green

Jeep station wagon with a police car's bar of red and blue lights and a couple of whip antennas bounced toward the river. A plume of dust boiled up behind the vehicle, then spread and settled into the surrounding woods.

Alone at the wheel of the Jeep was my sometime partner, Dave Finch. Today, as on every other day, the road meted out its daily increment of punishment to the Jeep's suspension and motor mounts and to Finch's lower spine and kidneys. From his right the two-way radio emitted the usual scratchy chorus of rangers and dispatchers outlining the progress of the repetitively mundane and gripping dramas of a summer weekend afternoon all the way down the river into the Central Valley. And as Finch fell deeper into the remove of the canyon, the voices on the radio became unintelligible bursts of static.

Three hundred feet above the river Finch crossed an invisible line bisecting the canyon wall at a perfect level. It had been two and a half decades since Congress had approved a dam that would flood this canyon. For a decade the partially built project had been at a standstill, stalemated by politics, budgets, and the complexities of the very rocks under its footings. Yet it had never officially been called off. So everything below that line—the gray pines and olive-drab oaks, the woolly sunflowers on the road's cutbank, the river, and even the little reservoir—could be seen only as temporary.

Finch came to the bottom of the road, and there he stopped and sat looking at the river with his tanned elbow out the open window of the idling Jeep. In front of him, on the cobble beach that sloped away to the lake and the river that flowed into it, dozens of cars were parked haphazardly—economy cars, older pickups, works in progress with bald tires, spots of primer and temporary registration stickers in their windows. Beyond them a small crowd of people lined the water's edge. Children splashed and squealed. Rough, tanned men—sheet metal workers, drywall installers, meatcutters, heavy-equipment operators, electricians' apprentices, carpenters, unemployed truck drivers, occupants of trailer houses in the hills and cheap apartments in little foothill towns—stood along the beach with beers in their hands. Women—grocery clerks, dental hygienists, auto-part store delivery drivers with little butterflies tattooed on their breasts and little roses on their thighs—stood waist-deep in the water in bright-colored bikini tops and cutoff jeans, or lay on towels smoothing suntan oil on their skin, or hovered over their children, puffing on cigarettes and gesturing animatedly to each other. Big dogs—pit bulls, rottweilers, and retrievers—barked at each other on the beach and made forays into the water for balls and sticks. The rhythmic bass of competing car stereos and the squeals of the children and the barking of the dogs echoed off the far canyon wall.

Somewhere in front of Finch an engine revved. He paid no attention to it. There was a clatter of cobbles and the dull clunk of rocks hitting a car's underbody, a flash of sunlight on steel and glass, and his eyes fixed on an older American sedan with dull paint rapidly gathering speed toward him through the parked cars, its rear end fishtailing and its tires smoking and hurling stones.

The car began to straighten out as it accelerated up the cobble strand. From one side a man appeared, running hard toward it. He was wild-haired, stripped to the waist, his face contorted and mouth open in a yell, the big veins and fibers of his neck standing out. He clutched an object in the crook of one arm like a football player running a ball. The other hand was raised in a fist, which he waved angrily as he ran at the car. As the car passed him, he lifted the ball and extended his throwing arm, firing the ball perfectly toward the car. It flew through the open passenger-side window and disappeared inside the speeding vehicle. Except it wasn't a football, Finch thought. Something larger. A beach ball, perhaps.

Then Finch thought, *No, not a beach ball.* It was something pink with limbs that moved as it flew through the air. *It's a baby that man just threw at that car. For the love of God, it's a baby,* he thought. Meanwhile the man continued to yell and shake his fist, running after the car, which still sped toward Finch.

Finch was not the only one whose attention was drawn to the commotion. As the baby sailed through the air, a low moan of horror and disbelief rose from the crowd on the beach, changing into a chorus of angry yells. As soon as they saw what he had done, several of the men and women down by the water rose to their feet and, unified by their hatred, began running toward the baby thrower. As if in slow motion, Finch was spinning the Jeep around to position himself for a traffic stop and reaching for the controls of the light bar and siren and the radio microphone from its clip on the dash. The man saw the mob coming at him. Finch unfastened his seat belt. The car, passing Finch's Jeep, braked to a stop. The driver's door flew open and a woman got out, screaming and waving her arms at Finch. Then she was reaching back into the car.

"Hey!" shouted Finch.

On the beach the mob descended upon the baby-thrower. Their aggregate intention now obvious to him, the man turned and ran at top speed down the beach along the lakeshore, disappearing into a thicket of willow and giant rush. The woman had pulled the baby from the car and was holding it up in front of her, then hugging it, then holding it up again, screaming, weeping, red-faced, screaming something at Finch, pointing in the direction of the man who had run away. Finch could not tell what she was saying. He had the radio mike now, and in his other hand he gripped the aluminum club he carried in his Jeep.

"Hey!" he yelled again at the woman, without knowing exactly what he wanted her to do, except to stop screaming so he could talk on the radio. Thumbing the microphone he said into it: "Northern, four six nine, I need code three backup at Upper Lake Clementine."

There was a short crackle of static from the speaker in the car and then nothing. Finch keyed the mike again. "Northern, four six nine, code three traffic."

"Four six nine, Northern," the dispatcher replied, sounding almost bored, "Please repeat your traffic."

"Northern four six nine. I need additional units to a four-fifteen at Upper Lake Clementine."

"Additional units . . . Lake Clementine . . ."

Finch imagined his backup roaring to the wrong end of the lake: "Negative, Northern—*Upper Lake, Upper Lake!*"

There was another burst of static. Then silence.

Finch: "Did you copy, Northern?"

Deafening static, then the dispatcher: "Copy, Upper Clementine, units available please respond."

"One seven nine," I said into my microphone several miles away. "Code three from the Confluence."

* * *

If the world exists in a perpetual state of uncertainty, if things are half-assed and watered-down and most things fall into a gray area, when you respond to a call like that you are bathed for a few minutes in superhuman certainty. You put away whatever squabbles you and your partners have had, ready to wade into the fray, to sacrifice yourself for any one of them. You hit the lights and siren and drive better than you normally do, think sharper than you normally do. The people in other cars look at you as you pass them on a mountain road, and at intersections the cars part for you like the Red Sea for Moses. It is an acceptable substitute for reality; it's fleeting, but it keeps you believing in what you do.

One after another, three other four-wheel-drive patrol trucks converged on the road and roared down it, arriving at the bottom with the brakes stinking and spongy under the pedal. I was a couple of minutes ahead of the others. I jerked my baton from where I kept it jammed between the seat back and cushion and rolled out of the car, sliding the club into the ring on my gun belt as I strode through the crowd now milling around Finch—fifty, perhaps seventy-five people.

Finch, poker-faced and sturdy in his green jeans, khaki shirt, gun belt, and green baseball cap with a badge insignia above the bill, stood by the open door of his Jeep with the woman. Her car was still parked where she had stopped it, the driver's door still open. Finch was asking her questions and taking notes on a clipboard. As I walked up to them he glanced at me and, without acknowledgment or greeting, began to speak with no trace of excitement other than the elevated volume of his voice and the pace of his delivery.

"This was a male-female fight. The guy—he's gone—ran downstream. They were arguing. She says when they decided to separate, one was going to leave with the car and the other would stay. Then there was more arguing about who got to take the car and who had to stay with the baby. She jumps in the car and tries to leave, and he runs after her. That's when I saw him throw the baby at her in the car. I thought it was a beach ball. Then I thought, *Shit—it's a baby*. Luckily it passed right in through the window."

"Where's the baby now?" I asked him.

He pointed to the shade of the willow trees next to us. "Those two women in the crowd offered to hold it."

I looked over at the trees. The baby was naked except for a paper diaper, face flushed, in the arms of a woman forty feet from where we were standing. She and another woman were making worried-looking ministrations over it.

"Is it okay? You wanna call an ambulance?" I asked.

"Seems okay. I've called Child Protective Services to pick the little guy up and have him checked at the hospital. Anyway—then the crowd turned on the man and I thought they were going to kill him. The guy saw what was about to happen to him and ran into the brush down there," Finch gestured toward the thickets down the beach. "That was a good twenty minutes ago and I have no idea where he is by now."

As Finch finished his account, the other rangers arrived, rumbling down the road in clouds of dust. Finch went back to questioning the woman. I walked over to where the others were just getting out of their rigs. They were surrounded by bystanders who wanted to tell them what had happened and demand that something be done. When I told them what Finch had told me, the rangers were only too happy to leave their petitioners and search for the missing suspect.

The way it worked with us, as soon as the adrenal part was over, someone would have to pay for all the fun. You paid by having to write the whole thing up, a process that could take an hour of note-taking in the field and several hours to a couple of days back at the ranger station. As a rule, the first ranger on the scene was the one who paid. You labored over your account of the incident, all the while knowing that the DA would flush most of the nefarious acts you described down the drain and deal the guy out on a felony specified as a misdemeanor. At sentencing, the judge would impose a suspended sentence because the jail was full, or maybe once he was out on bail the guy wouldn't bother to show up for his arraignment. A bench warrant would be issued, and when he got picked up a year and a half later on that and the seven other warrants he'd accumulated by then, expediency dictated that all of his cases be bound up and sold at a discount, and your charges might not even make the cut. So in the end he'd do a little jail time on some unrelated beef and no one would ever know what a beautiful job you'd done on the investigation. Year after year you wrote up these stories, and they'd wind up archived in a pile of cardboard boxes in the warehouse, flattening and drying like pressed flowers under the weight of all the stories above them—the unknown stratigraphy of your career.

In this case it was Finch who got to cut paper. To assist him while he continued taking the woman's statement, I began circulating to talk to the witnesses. The sweat ran down my face and fell in big brown dusty drops from my nose, staining my notes. My ballpoint pen refused to write on the wet spots. Our radios crackled with inarticulate static from Folsom Lake. The bystanders began to drift away, back down to the cool water.

It went on like this for a while. The whole affair had the usual combination of gripping danger and utter senselessness. Then I heard Finch on the little speaker-mike from the radio on my gun belt, clipped to the epaulet of my shirt: "One seven nine—that's the guy—long hair—no shirt—walking toward us."

I looked at Finch. He was pointing to a lanky man with unkempt hair walking up the sandy track from the willow thickets. The remaining spectators around us began to yell: "That's him! Aren't you going to do anything? That's the guy who tried to kill her baby!" I took a few steps toward the man, placing myself between him and the angry bystanders. He wore only dirty athletic shoes and a pair of cutoff jeans. He looked dazed.

"Put your hands up," I commanded him, pulling my baton from its ring. I didn't brandish it. Instead, cocking my wrist, I aligned it along the back of my forearm, where it wasn't threatening but was instantly ready.

"Turn around. Interlace your fingers and put your hands behind your head. Spread your legs. Don't move." I stepped around behind the man and patted the pockets of his shorts for weapons. Then I handcuffed him and, leading him over to my Jeep, put him in the backseat behind the expanded-metal prisoner cage. His sweaty back made a muddy smear across the dusty vinyl of the seat back. He looked weary. He said nothing and avoided my eyes. I didn't question him. He wasn't going anywhere, and now that he was captive, he had to be read his rights. I was more eager to question the witnesses on the beach before they disappeared, so I left him in the Jeep with the air conditioner on full blast and went back to work on our notes and interviews. A breeze off the river stirred the leaves on the willow trees and momentarily cooled me, blowing through my sweat-soaked shirt on my belly, below my bulletproof vest. This thing was pretty well over.

Twenty minutes later I had my part of the statement-taking done. I returned to the Jeep to drop off a page full of notes and get a drink of water. Glancing at the prisoner in the back, I saw him slumped over sideways. I took off my sunglasses and studied his face. It was blue, ashen blue, like a dead man's. He was absolutely motionless.

"Finch! Look at this!"

Finch walked over and peered at the man through the side window of the car.

"He's faking it," he said.

"The hell he is."

"He's faking it."

"I don't know how he could fake that color. Take a look."

I opened the door and leaned into the backseat. I put my hand on the man's clammy chest, feeling for movement. Holding my face cautiously close to his, I listened for breathing. "Nothing," I told Finch over my shoulder. "He's not breathing."

"Shit," said Finch.

I reached for the latch on the man's seatbelt. Grabbing his feet, I dragged them up off the floor. He was dead weight. I pulled on his legs. Finch shoved in next to me and grabbed one foot. The man tumbled out of the car onto his back on the rocky beach.

Kneeling on the rocks next to the still body I rolled the tips of the index and middle fingers of my right hand down off the prominence of the man's Adam's apple to the carotid artery, feeling for a pulse. Finch was on the radio calling for an ambulance. "His heart is still beating," I told Finch.

I jumped up and ran around to the back of the Jeep, opened the
tailgate, opened the equipment box inside, and jerked out the
medic's pack and oxygen kit. I ran back around the Jeep, put them
down, ripped open their cases, and cranked open the oxygen supply
valve. The regulator made a reassuring hiss and the gauge spiked up.
I pulled on a pair of surgical gloves. I reached into the medic's kit
for an airway, sized it against the man's clammy jaw, discarded it for
another, opened his mouth gingerly with a finger and thumb, and
threaded the curved plastic tube over his blue tongue and down his
throat. Finch was uncoiling the shiny green supply line for the
demand valve and handed the valve to me. I hit the button once: it
made a satisfying *shush*. I picked up a mask from the kit and press-
fitted it onto the valve, pushed it over the man's mouth and nose,
and began to breathe him. Dispatch called; our ambulance was en
route. I reached for the speaker-mike and acknowledged their
transmission.

For half an hour, maybe forty minutes, I watched his chest rise
and fall in response to the oxygen I forced into it with the button
under my thumb. Periodically I'd stop to check for a pulse. His heart
was still beating. Weak, but beating. With Finch and the other
rangers to keep an eye on the crowd, my world got very small and
simple, just the *sshhush* of the demand valve, the still body, and
rounded river rocks beneath it.

Around the body were cobbles of greenstone the color of jade,
and granite ones with sparkling salt-and-pepper crystals. There
were river-rounded schists, the alternating layers of black-and-
white minerals across their rounded flanks like stripes on a zebra.
There were charcoal-gray gabbros. There were tan quartzites in
which more wear-resistant veins of quartz or calcite stood out in
bas-relief, branching like the blue veins on the still man's pale
arms. There were eggs of porphyry the color of dried blood and orbs
of milky quartz blasted by nineteenth-century gold miners from
fossil riverbeds high on the canyon walls upstream, where they'd
lain entombed for fifty million years since those rivers had been
buried by volcanic eruptions. Back in the living world now, these
stones were orphans, because the mountains from which those
ancient rivers had plucked them had long ago been washed down to

the sea. Each rock and its texture, each lungful of oxygen, each moment, and then each next moment—these are all life is made of when nothing else can be counted on. And for this reason there is a strange peacefulness at the center of catastrophe.

After a while, the man's face began to pink up. His limbs twitched. The airway I'd put down his throat begin to bob and click against the interior of the clear plastic oxygen mask. He was coming to, and as he did, his gag reflex was coming back. Quickly I lifted the mask and pulled the airway out of him so it wouldn't cause him to vomit and inhale his stomach contents, which could lead to pneumonia that might kill him slowly later, if he didn't die before the ambulance got there. His eyelids fluttered. He took a couple of ragged breaths, and then another. Then there was nothing. Then another breath. Then nothing.

He had stopped breathing again. Again I inserted the airway and began moving his air for him. It went on like this, two, then three times.

One of the other rangers stood over us, watching. The mob had gathered in a circle around us. "Is he dead?" a woman asked. "I hope so," some guy answered.

There were needle tracks on the man's arms. When he had run away, he must have gone in the bushes and fixed himself up with a speedball—a heroin and methamphetamine cocktail.

"Where's the damn ambulance?" I asked Finch, watching the man's chest deflate for the umpteenth time and glancing at the declining pressure gauge on my O2 tank. *It'll be harder to keep him alive if I run out of oxygen,* I thought. I heard Finch calling dispatch for a status on the ambulance.

Eventually, the ambulance got there. The other rangers moved the crowd of bystanders out of the way. A man and a woman in dark blue jumpsuits took over my patient, placing him on a gurney while I continued breathing him. Then, when they were ready, I pulled my mask off and they replaced it with theirs. We exchanged paperwork rapidly, and they loaded and went up the road, their amber and red lights blinking through the trail of dust behind them.

I stood, put my hands on my aching lower back, and arched backward to stretch. My knees were sore from the rocks, a thing I hadn't noticed until now. I looked over at Finch and grinned, shaking my head. "Faking it, huh?"

"Yeah, well . . . ," he shrugged his shoulders, grinned. I shrugged, grinned back.

With the adrenaline wearing off came the weariness, the dry mouth, the hunger. I drank a quart of water from the Jeep. I picked up my medical kit, equipment, bits of gauze, and green rubber surgical gloves off the rocks, tried to dust off my green jeans, found a bandanna and wiped the muddy sweat from my face. In a few minutes I heard the ambulance hit the Foresthill Road, where its siren came on. The wail echoed off the canyon walls above us for a period of minutes, then grew fainter and trailed away down the Foresthill Divide.

Back at our ranger station fifty feet below the waterline of the Auburn Dam in the lower North Fork canyon, I let myself into the front room that had once been the kitchen of the firefighters' mess and now functioned as our combination locker room, lunchroom, and secondary office. I flicked on the switch by the door. The cool fluorescents blinked and buzzed to life. I slumped into one of the old oak chairs around the big table in the center of the room, kicked my feet up on the table, reached for the phone, and dialed the number for the ER at the little hospital in Auburn. As the line rang I flipped open my lunchbox, unwrapped a sandwich, and took a bite. A nurse answered the phone. I told her I wanted to check on a patient we had sent in and gave her the man's name.

"I'll let you talk to the doctor about that. He's right here," she said. She put the phone on hold.

I took another bite of the sandwich, leafing distractedly through a stack of wanted fugitive bulletins and be-on-the-lookouts on the table.

The doctor came on: a guy I knew. I told him I was calling to see if my man made it.

"Yeah, he's fine. It was an overdose. We're running bloods, but

I'd say from the agitated behavior followed by the loss of interest in breathing it's probably some mixture of heroin and a stimulant like cocaine or crank. Anyway, from what the medics said, you guys did a great job—"

"Oh—"

"—and I got a little from them about what our guy had done before he coded, you know? So it looks like you've saved his miserable life. I guess that should make you happy." I thanked him and hung up, took another bite of the sandwich, leaned back in the chair, and stared up at the pale yellow paint on the pine planks of the ceiling.

"There are no innocent victims in this place," Finch always said as we watched the same people appear in alternating roles over the years. One day your guy was a perpetrator; a week or a year later he was a victim. Five years and a couple more tattoos later, you arrested him again as a perpetrator. Eventually he might wind up dead, drowned in the river or killed in a car crash or shot by one of his peers, and you listed him in the blank on the report where it said "victim."

The exception was an innocent like the Beach Ball Baby, as Finch was to call him from time to time when we would recount the story over the gales of laughter that were always our substitute for ennui. Then again, by now that little boy must be well into high school, and if his life turned out as badly as it began, he may already have qualified for a juvenile offender record, an obituary, or both.

But I like to think not. I like to think he got lucky, got placed with foster parents who loved him and lavished the good things on him. Perhaps he'll be valedictorian of his senior class and grow up to be a teacher, social worker, political reformer—who knows, maybe even a ranger.

I am less sanguine about his father's prospects. By saving him I set him loose again upon the world and, God help me, perhaps upon that little boy, unless of course the courts did their job—and when could that ever be counted on? But you never know. Perhaps there was some purpose served by that man's survival, some good he would do later to redeem himself. By the time of the Beach Ball Baby I was beginning to tell myself things like that. In any case, a park ranger is a protector. You protect the land from the people, the people from the land, the people from each other, and the people from themselves. It's what you are trained to do without even thinking, a reflexive and unconditional act. If you're lucky, you get assigned to people who seem worth saving and land and waters whose situation is not hopeless. If not, you save them anyway. And maybe in time, saving them will make them worth it.

in the home of the heart

David Lukas

Before I could even read I started studying wild animals and memorizing their pictures in field guides. Throughout my childhood I dreamed of owning a zoo, sailing to the Galápagos, launching expeditions in hopes of discovering new species. I collected, experimented, cataloged, and took field notes at an age when other kids cared more about playing on the playground; I guess I was destined to be a naturalist.

And like many other young naturalists I revered those white-haired naturalists of old—sharp-eyed sages like Darwin and Wallace who journeyed fearlessly around the globe, making astute observations and thinking grand thoughts about nature. I clung to these images because I grew up in small fishing towns on the Oregon coast and was hungry for heroes who mirrored my love of the natural world.

Throughout my adult life I continued on this path: traveling widely in Borneo, Peru, and Central America to study exotic ecosystems, working on biological research projects all over the western United States, writing extensively about the natural world, and leading hundreds of nature walks and tours. Although I may not be a white-haired old sage like my heroes, I have been deeply embedded in the naturalist's tradition for nearly forty years. I have studied the naturalist's world from all angles and have met all types of people in this field, joining them on the walks they were leading and reading books they have written.

People in Western cultures have long relied on naturalists as their primary guides in the natural world, counting on them to observe, document, and bring news of nature to the larger culture. Naturalists are the ones who tell us stories about plants and animals, write field guides, teach classes, and lead us on walks—all in the tradition established by Darwin and other early naturalists.

As a naturalist I meet amazing people every day with tremendous enthusiasm and compassion for the natural world, but at the same time I see a world in staggering decline: rain forests that I once roamed being cut, seafood that I once relished nearly wiped out or loaded with mercury, and field after field from my childhood being swallowed in housing tracts. I would call these urgent times.

In the face of this paradox it is worth asking whether naturalists are up to the task of guiding us through the perils of the modern world and its breathtaking destruction of the natural environment.

I would say that yes, naturalists are up to the task, but that the role of the naturalist needs to be questioned and redefined. In the same way that I did as a child, all of us emulate and uphold to one degree or another the archetypal image of the naturalist (though, thankfully, many women now fill the ranks of great naturalists). Times have changed, but the role of the naturalist, or our image of the role of the naturalist, seems to be lagging behind.

I have never questioned my own career, but perhaps it is time to acknowledge that the famous naturalists of yesteryear were deeply embedded in the grand metaphors of their time—namely, exploration and conquest—and that we have unconsciously continued to replicate these themes in our own thinking about the natural world: go forth and discover, capture through observation, tame with description, and return with the triumph of knowledge and mastery over the wild unknown.

This is not to say these themes are a mistake; in fact many species have been discovered and ecological principles revealed under the aegis of these themes. I make this point because I believe these themes limit our idea of what a naturalist can be. I would like to see naturalists stretch beyond these old boundaries.

Unfortunately, in many ways the opposite seems to be occurring. What remains of the naturalist's tradition has been largely reduced to rote memorization of taxonomic classification and routine biological concepts. It is as if the naturalist's role has morphed into little more than going out and naming objects in nature. Birdwatchers do this in making lists of the birds they see on their field trips, and naturalists do it when they identify plants and animals for participants on a nature walk.

The question arises for me whether this old, and still extant, understanding of the naturalist's role is enough for our urgent times. Is it enough to merely capture and identify while the figurative palace is burning; or can naturalists, as caretakers of our journey into the natural world, fulfill a unique responsibility to forge a new path?

Over the past year I have been unexpectedly asked to do a tremendous amount of work around grief and personal growth, and in the course of reading the voluminous literature on this subject I have come to realize that the grand metaphors of our time have in fact shifted dramatically. What may have once been expressed as "explore and conquer" is now better stated as "home, health, and relationship."

As a society we grapple daily with the shallow mockery of advertising, the devious schemes of politicians and business leaders, and the empty promises of capitalism. Our fractured communities and livelihoods leave many of us with a sense of hollowness bordering on the clinical. As individuals we struggle to make ends meet and to understand this complex world. Yet I walk the empty streets of my neighborhood at night and see entire families isolated around the blue glow of televisions in each living room, as if everyone has collectively given up hope.

It is a terrible backdrop against which the naturalist sets to work. The environment is being cut to pieces and the future looks grim. People are distracted, anxious, and isolated from one another. It is hard sometimes to get people to think about the natural world or to understand what a naturalist is trying to communicate.

Yet I think part of the problem is that naturalists have tacitly accepted the language of nature proposed by the larger society. We study nature, we talk about nature, we watch nature, and we even engage in nature writing. In contrast, indigenous cultures rarely (if ever) possess a word for nature, not even recognizing it as a distinct concept. What is "nature" if not a way of delineating Other and making it separate from ourselves? And once separated from Other what choice do we have but to be lonely voyeurs?

I am not privy to the reasons why indigenous cultures do not have a label "nature," but my intuition and life experience tell me there is no such thing as nature; there is only home. And in light of this I would suggest that the true role of the naturalist is to guide people into the home of the heart.

It may not be a coincidence that this same intuition is even reflected in the word "ecology." Derived from the Greek *oikos*, "home or house," it translates literally as "the study of home." And by definition it is the study of relationships. If not already implied, health cannot be far behind.

As an antidote to the pain and fracturing experienced in my own life, I now prefer to speak of home and healthy relationship. And I wonder why a naturalist could not do the same in teaching people about nature, especially because the very roots of ecology employ the same language.

It is valuable to begin by acknowledging that the names and concepts naturalists use are but windows onto a much larger reality. I often feel this way when I'm leading a walk, that when I point out a white-crowned sparrow I am barely touching the tip of a giant iceberg—that this thing so easily encapsulated in a small name has a rich life beyond the grasp of my words. I long for a way to shift myself and the group into a much deeper vision, to no longer be spectators sneaking peeks through tiny windows but to fully enter the home of the heart.

To truly comprehend the lives of these creatures would require a new way of seeing and knowing. Although naturalists are master observers, trained by a lifetime of close scrutiny and curiosity, I can speak from experience in saying that something is missing here. Working from Jung's description of the four ways we perceive the world, ecopsychologist Rich Silver talks about utilizing "sensing, feeling, imagining, and knowing" as ways to enter the natural world.

When I look at an animal, or have a group watch an animal, I know that I'm focusing on visual perception, a form of sensing, almost to the exclusion of any other type of perception. Wouldn't it be amazing to lead a group in the other four directions as well?

In teaching a class or leading a walk, the naturalist is responsible for cultivating a sacred space, both within the group, and between the participants and the natural world. And when I speak of sacred space, I am not speaking merely of a spiritual dimension but also of a moral and emotional field in which people feel trust, security, and companionship.

I have found that this asks for an extraordinary degree of attention and care. The task demands several things at once, including setting aside the ego so as to speak *from* nature, intuitively and without conceit, rather than speaking *about* nature. To this I would add the obligation of learning the language of the heart so that the naturalist can recognize values of hope, love, forgiveness, and respect at every scale from the pore on a mushroom cap to global crisis.

These tasks are important because the naturalist often works with people who have little experience or comfort in the natural world and who feel the awkwardness of being strangers to this place.

In response I find myself turning to a very personal place. Rather than identifying "this tree as a bay laurel," I might say "the first time I met this tree was when I moved to California in 1991, and it has become my sign of strength and determination in the face of aloneness." By adding his or her personal experience, the naturalist may immediately signal to the group that the door has been opened to the private, mythic realm that is seldom invited on public nature walks. This is the realm, of whatever color and character, that each person holds within, a realm of fantasy, insecurity, or hope that is not readily shared. By example, the naturalist reveals and establishes a safe place for the emergence of an authentic inner vulnerability that each person hides within.

To this mix the naturalist begins weaving in stories from the scientific literature, carefully choosing tidbits of knowledge that deepen the group's perception of the natural world. Although concepts like nutrient uptake, niche partitioning, and clutch size may

seem obtuse at first glance, in the hands of a skilled naturalist they
capture the attention like a hawk seizing a mouse. I am not being
specious in speaking of storytelling this way. Each summer I lead
nature walks at the Squaw Valley Community of Writers, an annual
writers' workshop held in the Sierra Nevada. People come to the
workshop from all corners of the country and with many back-
grounds, but there is always a shared moment on the trail when all
extraneous conversation stops and we talk about things like mycor-
rhizal fungi and how trees are simply solar antennae that collect
sunlight energy to feed an underground web of life.

I once had the pleasure of leading a group of corporate execu-
tives on a walk at a retreat in coastal California. They were a difficult
group to say the least; they were discourteous, impatient, and
impossible to focus while I tried to introduce them to the natural
world—that is until I explained to them the obscure behavior of
apophallation, the way in which slugs chew each other's penises off.
Like kids sharing a nasty joke, they became giddy with excitement
and had no problem paying close attention for the next two hours.

One of the most honorable acts of the naturalist's profession is
taking time to walk the landscape before leading a group there, to
ask the land, "What do you want me to teach this group?" And at the
same time asking your own spirit, "How may I best tell this story
today?"

This is not a facile undertaking, for it requires the deepest levels
of attention and inquiry possible. It is a time for silent walking and
close observation: It is a form of meditation. Personally I pay particular attention to the land's expression of life, both in the near term,
as in which birds are singing and which flowers are blooming, but
also to longer cycles like the stages of forest succession, decay, and
growth. I also listen closely for my own interior energy, asking how
deeply I want to reach into my reservoir of stories, pondering which
themes to bring forward, wondering how I will connect people to
place.

It is an awesome responsibility to stand before a group of
strangers and propose to guide them into an experience of the natural world. Leading a group in this context is a delicate juggling act
between summoning curiosity, listening openly to people's stories,

and maintaining the flow of the program. No naturalist does this perfectly every time, but the challenges of this unpredictable balancing act are what keep the job so exciting. I remember one memorable walk trying to juggle this complex dynamic with a large group that included three notably unhappy, undisciplined youngsters dropped off by parents who thought the nature walk was a great way to get free child care. I found this fascinating because the other participants on the walk were irritated by the unruly children, but over time became increasingly intrigued by their observations and questions. The children too calmed down and began to pay attention to what the group was looking at.

I have found that it is very important to listen to people's stories with kindness and care, and to call forth questions hidden by shyness or aggressive voices. Asking people to speak their names and interests out loud, for instance, is one way to help bring a group together.

Although a naturalist uses tools like these to open people's hearts, he or she is not a babysitter or therapist. The naturalist's primary job is to open up a larger dialogue, and this is perhaps the harder task in front of a group, to invite the presence of Other into the conversation. Without this presence, people will start thinking that the stories and questions are about them, when in fact the program is not about *you* but about *community*, not about *nature* but about *home*. My corporate executive group, for example, gleefully shifted their discussion from corporate concerns to the Other without even realizing they were participating in a different kind of dialogue.

It is possible to draw Other into the conversation by gently handling creatures that people are mostly afraid of, or to unfold the exquisite components of a flower, or to tell a story so breathtaking and unique that people momentarily forget who they are. And the secret, as in any good conversation, is to continue building on these introductory comments by extending the dialogue further and further.

The best example from my own walks is the time we found a tiny brilliant orange mushroom along the trail at Point Reyes National Seashore. As our group of about twenty adults passed the mushroom around the circle, examining it closely with a hand lens, the two

leaders talked about the structure of mushrooms and their life history. Only when the mushroom reached the last person in the circle
did someone realize that on the tiny mushroom was a cold little
aphid, so the mushroom and its hitchhiker made another circuit
around the circle as the conversation went to new levels. Then when
the topic appeared exhausted and people began getting ready to walk
again, I discovered that on the *knee* of the little aphid on the tiny
mushroom was a mite sucking the aphid's blood! Of course everyone
wanted to see and talk about this, and when all was said and done
that tiny mushroom completely occupied our group's attention for a
good forty-five minutes and it was hard to return to our normal perspective on the world.

I have found in this way that the inclusion of Other into the conversation begins to create a sense of community, a place where all
voices are welcomed and heard, a place where even the small and
timid have equal standing with the large and mighty. The inclusion
of Other is a novel step for many people because our society is
spoon-fed so many lies about fear and terrorism, not to mention
fairy tales about fighting and conquering the Other rather than
greeting and inquiring into things we do not understand. In my
experience groups readily begin to mirror this dynamic of inclusion,
conversation, and community as a nature walk moves along. And in
mirroring this dynamic, people notably relax and begin speaking
and listening from their hearts.

This alone would be a tremendous accomplishment for any naturalist or for any nature walk, but I suspect that the frontier can be
pushed to deeper levels, perhaps to levels our society does not have
language for yet. There is, for instance, a kind of awareness recognized by some Eastern traditions where perception of reality no
longer resides in the brain but is an activity of the totality of the
body. What could it be like to perceive a mite on the knee of an
aphid with something more than your mind and vision? And what
would happen if this perception spontaneously opened up your
heart and encouraged you to become an active citizen in your own
community?

I am often asked on walks if the fantastic stories and facts I tell
are true, as if truth were the only significant measure of an experience. It must be a by-product of our culture that we obsess on

factual accuracy rather than on whether a story is honest and authentic. My belief is that the role of a naturalist is to be a good storyteller and to tell honest stories well. It is always about stories and mythology anyway, whether you are a scientist, doctor, shaman, priest, or naturalist. Our duty is to tell stories that put people's lives in order, stories that work for the age you live in—stories that properly honor the realms of logic, heart, and right relations.

In this work the natural world is not Other, lurking out there beyond the perimeter of our precious civilized mind; it is home, our only home, and we reside entirely within it. Our task, as it always has been, is to exercise care. Here is the place where we open our hearts, inquire deeply, and gain the grace to treat each other with respect.

prairie interrupted

SHELLEY ARMITAGE

. . . the term landscape, as it has entered the English language, is mis-
leading. "A portion of territory the eye can comprehend in a single
view" does not correctly describe the relationship between the human
being and his or her surroundings. This assumes the viewer is somehow
outside or *separate from* the territory he or she surveys. Viewers are as
much a part of the landscape as the boulders they stand on.

LESLIE MARMON SILKO

It has always reminded me of the benign sloping back of a bron-
tosaurus, this prairie. Gray green, in deepening or waxing shades
depending on the time of year, this modest drainage to the Canadian
River, near the border of northwest Texas and New Mexico, cleaves,
leaving rounded backs of earth on either side. I guess you'd say I feel
I can pet them, stroke them as you would some creature wild and
exotic but tolerating your graces. *A child's pleasant memory,
dinosaurs—that enthusiasm one of our childhood rites of passage.* I link
it to my familiarity with a place Pleistocene-like, yet young in
human history.

Perhaps it's the stimulation of imagining oneself in relationship to
something that old, something that was once ocean, that draws me.
And immense. A place you can lose yourself in. These Rolling Plains
of Texas are a small branch of the Texas High Plains, which stretch
hundreds of miles, forming one of the largest plateaus in North
America. Unlike the desert places where I've lived, El Paso, Doña
Ana, and Bernalillo counties in New Mexico, which visibly suggest
dried upstart beds, former coral reefs—an ocean's skeleton
exposed—this northernmost Texas prairie is covered. It's that sea of
grass written dismissively and also beguilingly about in expeditionary chronicles and other accounts. It's also a wanderer's place,

historically formidable because arid, a region people often tried to cross quickly to get somewhere else. These stories, records, personal perspectives, boomers' reports are by-products of an initial experiential moment calling for image-making, records more of human perspectives than the prairie itself.

Still, what can humans do but make texts—documents, representations? The photographer Robert Adams once remarked to me that if nineteenth-century landscape photography was about silence, twentieth-century landscape photography was about noise. Accordingly, a silent look now is impossible. Looking must be of the Don DeLillo type, a visualized "white noise." Adams's own photographs, connected at one point with a group called the "New Topographics," picture plastic bags caught on Rocky Mountain Front Range cacti, the tire tracks of ATVs marking what once was open range. Adams's observation is ironic because the silence we associate with pristine nature instead contained its own noisy natural sounds, today absent or drowned out by the modern buzz of the built environment. Those nineteenth-century photographs, say of the Sierras, were, above all, a studied effort to fix a silence that only the mute photograph can. Who knows about O'Sullivan's or Watkins's actual western experience? It's the art that hushes. My repeated prairie walks, Interstate 40 to my south, with a southwesterly wind pushing me, make the experience of the "natural world" that of the constant din of truck traffic. I've gotten so used to it, I don't know the difference. Unrelenting presence, America's first military transit highway creates its own wind, a steady rush of air buzzing just above the horizon line. In the 1950s the interstate replaced the now nostalgically celebrated Route 66, which was the first modern roadway to cut through the southern prairie of Armitage Farms, our farm and ranch, where I regularly walk. Both followed older expeditionary routes, Native American crossings, and game trails that heeded the logic of geography and water.

But what scuttles beside, below, and above me as I walk, that other commerce of the prairies? What teeming inheritors of the Pleistocene-cum-prairie persist in their unseen movements, their instinctive compasses? This prairie has been interrupted, after all, by drought cycles, one-way plowing, conservation belts, terracing, the first barbed-wire fences, overgrazing, as well as the digging of persistent badgers who can bring down a fence in no time. Perhaps it makes more sense to admit that such disturbances, human and natural, are all mixed up, each with their inherent order, for when you look at this groundswell of varied soils, for instance, it reads like slighted and dismembered documents—shapes of time that belie intervention.

We humans construct chronicles as a wish to see time as sequential, somehow adding up. We photograph and map and name. Just in my lifetime, a new county road was cut north from I-40, forming one border of our place. On the south side, where the Santa Fe Railroad tracks were removed, new fences reclaimed old track beds, and later satellite photographs provided the Social Conservation Service offices with images of places they number "Farm 366" and "Farm 184." Perhaps more fitting a prairie so interrupted would be the scientific notion of time as a series of confluences or as intuitive roadways—more like the sense of our childhood meanderings than the foldout maps of our adult years.

In a place—the apparent flat short-grass prairie—which begs a horizontal viewing as a reasonable perspective, I am reminded of a painting I saw recently of beach and oceanfront life. The painter reframed the viewer's expectations, the perspective narrowed and from above, enforcing a vertical orientation instead. Beach and ocean met vertical sky, canceling the usual languorous horizontal touristy view. Why not consider animal presence vertically as well? Yesterday's porcupine, which I saw years ago in the farm's last standing cottonwood tree, napping during the daytime, lolling on a thick limb, has a den somewhere underground. His nocturnal ramblings take him to weed and water sources, the bark of the large cottonwood completely stripped in his lifetime. He sleeps above its naked remains. Winter takes him deep again, vertical, sleeping below as he slept above, having adjusted to the prairie as treeless reality. Perhaps the single old cottonwood was a dream come true, his mammal imagination letting him ride high for a few seasons until he had to avoid the cracked and dangerous limb of his own voraciousness—the death of his dream aboveground.

I saw him later, arthritic, exaggeratedly ambling from side to side, literally rocking down the road. Like so many animals at the farm, he crosshatched the area connecting feeding grounds to water sources. He had become horizontal again in his adaptations. And most recently I spotted him at the roadside, stripping kosher weed stalks as if they were the bark of a tree. He manages his vertical dreams on a different scale.

Bordering this same county road, the bar ditch had long been home, and breeding and nesting ground, for a number of species. Here, because of water runoff, a depth that holds moisture, even snow, and the benignity of the neighbor farmers who tend to the land inside the barbed-wire fence but not out, varieties of the mixed prairie persist year after year. Such cover may be home of prairie box turtles repeating their amphibian habits, unaware of trucks that are larger and faster by the year. Given the low statistics of the annually laid eggs that survive natural predators, these turtles are particularly lucky to be alive in the postindustrial world. When I find one crossing the gravel and caliche road, I want to hurry her across. And cross she must! Such internal notion of place becomes a replacing of breeding and feeding grounds despite the raised road beds. More often than not I find a dead turtle, pale diamond green shell smashed by one of those trucks, a flattened abstract design. Now here is, ironically, a "silent" nature, which allows close examination of the shell, the head, the claws digging into death. I ask myself: *When does a prairie become a pasture? Old animal trails speedy thoroughfares? Green notions domesticated?*

Other perspectives of prairie life, for example aerial views, suggest a confluence of such interruptions or interventions, a pattern in the flattening of time as aerial photographs, for example, map contiguous space. The cultural geographer J. B. Jackson, editor of the early periodical *Landscape*, initiated such revelations in his cultivation of the documentary art of aerial photography. Once flying in a private plane over the farm and grassland, I experienced this perspective. I could see the conservation terraces built in the 1930s. I could also see they were built along a small series of leveled areas, like small plateaus, faintly different in color, suggesting different soil types. Later, on the ground, I discovered a cache of old photo-

graphs made in the same area, showing that the pasture I had seen
from above had been part of an early Oldham County golf course. In
the same manner that turn-of-the-century settler Doc Lloyd printed
brochures advertising Oldham Country as the "garden" of the panhandle, local boosters believed they could attract settlers to the town
of Vega by building their own links. Sand greens were plotted on the
upslopes on either side of the prevalent draw on our place a few
years before my dad bought the land. In an early 1930s photograph,
local men with their scruffy clubs and bags chip golf balls out of a
sand green. Conditions for play during the first Dust Bowl years
must have made the sand greens ironic reminders of disappearing
topsoil. I do wonder about that sand. Had it formed some soil basis
in what is now another prairie mix, that varied soil and vegetation
color so visible from my flight?

It has taken a half century for the firmly grounded local farmers
to envision putting down manure for "natural" fertilization, to bring
back the tractored-out soil and overgrazed grasses of the depression
and the drought cycles. Cattle accomplish a measure of this, but they
trample the grasses and crops and disrupt the seed cycles. Buffalo
previously did indeed roam, leaving nourishing excrement behind,
but also, because of their movement, allowed for the natural replen-
ishment of grasses. I have been watching an old buffalo wallow still
visible in a corner of the south pasture, near the tilled land. Through
the years I see its basin deepen and form the beginnings of a wash
that eventually will break down through wind and water erosion to
form yet another route to the river, taking a part of the prairie with
it.

Other more modern projects, like the dams along the central
draw of this prairie, have done little to stop the persistence of water
and topographic change. On our farm, the dam built up to make a
stock tank in the late 1920s, shortly after the prairie was first broken out for wheat farming in the panhandle, lasted awhile but collapsed in one of the high rises late in that decade.

By the time I was old enough to go to the farm with my dad and
grandfather, I thought of both sides of the broken dam as mountains
(another dinosaur fantasy? another child's playground?)—never in

the practical ways they did. Later, the CCC guys built a dam of rocks hauled from the Canadian River back upstream. Another conservation effort during the 1930s, it has long been eroded by water forming around it a deeper willful channel. During the occasional rains the bottom of this old dam fills, though. Once it rained so much that there were catfish pouring over the dam from another tank up the draw. During that same strong storm one of our neighbor's iron potbellied stoves washed from his cattle camp down to the Canadian River.

The final attempt to dam the draw was my dad's, who as an amateur engineer, and with his old Massey tractor, constructed a dirt dam above the CCC washout. That too proved folly in a country given to extremes. He stocked it with catfish and even rigged a feeder that he could cast out into the middle of the lakelike waters in the wet years. The tank alternately was dry and full for a few years, the catfish digging way down into the subterranean wetness until that too cracked and broke the chain. My dad died of a heart attack one weekend when he was shoring up sections of the cracked dam. He was lifting, moving large rocks. Days later I picked up a very small stone from the site to keep with me as if I could hold his time in my hand.

Just a mile from this pasture, two other landowners have tended their water in different ways, the latest with a fancy holding tank. This was the same rancher who decided to clear the mesquite and cholla cactus from the prairie and cross-fence it ostensibly for a mother cow/calf operation. To make a prairie only promoted more loss of habitat; the lack of cover allowed for topsoil wash. Loss of original plant diversity changed the late summer arrival of the usual monarch butterfly population. That and consistent mowing of the bar ditches up and down this section compromised the natural nesting places for turtles and meadowlarks and other creatures. From the bar ditches the larks once colored the sky with their mating calls, a rainbow of sound arching the country road. Nesting habitat compromised, they are singular, largely silent. Up the road, the other neighbor never turns off his windmill. Water spills over the cattle tub, a waste, but its coursing runoff attracts seasonal avocets and the springtime's dancing sandhill cranes.

* * *

In March 2005, I was in Kailua, Hawaii, at a friend's house, when I
read an e-mail from my longtime family friend, Ann Haliburton,
eighty-five, about the panhandle prairie fires. Life by the ocean
seemed a long way from the mainland, but in particular from the
Texas drought and the shock of fire. Another interruption.

With mauka rains tinkling on the ti leaves, windows flush in
undulating greens, the salty smell of the ocean nearby, I tried to
imagine fire. By sheer will I wanted to put out those distant fires. I
feared visualizing my home prairie with sizzling ground noise,
choking smoke, the unpredictable rage of crackling heat. The
bunching of cattle, the need to cut fences, the rolling eyes of livestock replaced the seeming soft, rolling prairie I carried always
inside me when away. I was in the tropics surrounded by water! I
went online. I tried to read more. I held positive thoughts that did
not have fire in them. Next day I read a report in the *Honolulu Adver-
tiser* on the still uncontained grass fire already engulfing sixty thousand acres near Amarillo, Texas. It was a major national disaster
story but mostly lost in the wake of Katrina and front-page war
news.

My adult life had been one of such disconnections, chosen interruptions. Shouldn't my "lifestyle" have prepared me for this? Yes, I
spent my childhood through high school in Vega, Texas, the middle
of the prairie, as the town name indicates. But I had been traveling
ever since—college elsewhere, professional stints in New Mexico,
Tennessee, Hawaii, grants in New York State, the Northwest, conferences all over the United States, Fulbrights in Eritrea, Portugal,
Hungary, Poland, and Finland. Mostly I had been in urban places, in
cities with a coastline, or a river or lake nearby. Like most kids
reared in rural areas who leave home to make their lives elsewhere,
I initially tried to replace the rural prairie life with something the
outside world told me was "better."

I had returned regularly—summers, holidays, for another job in
the area. Meanwhile, the prairie remained inside, a grounding in
my wanderings. Gradually, I came to see some continuities in supposedly unrelated places. I remember when I first moved into the
Chihuahuan Desert, living on an escarpment ten miles northwest of

El Paso, that one morning I awoke to see dense fog covering the farming valley of the Rio Grande below. In the distance were the Franklin Mountains, which run through the center of El Paso. The effect stunned me as it appeared to be the same view I had from my apartment off Lanikai near Kailua on Oahu where two green islands rise out of that aqua ocean. The valley fog looked like that Pacific fog; the Franklin tops exactly like the two island peaks. I felt perched on the backbone of metaphor, that transitory link of ocean and desert, the insides and outsides of my life.

Earth, air, fire, water. How basic the composition of our bodies within the world's body. The earliest book I remember attempting to read as a child was *The World We Live In*. I still have it in my library. Fascinated by its survey of the great geologic periods, the flora and fauna of certain of the earth's eras, the cataclysms that changed them, I imagined myself stepping into the illustrated diorama of scientific chapter and verse. But the science of that 1950s book did not invite an understanding of continuities. Later I discovered that folklorists studying dreams in the 1970s identified survivals, remnants of the past, recurring as elements in the accounts of dreams. Apparently, embedded in the unconscious were recognizable kernels—elements of longer narratives, recurring symbols, cultural remnants. These kernels referenced portions of older supposedly lost cultural stories; they were identified as snippets that could potentially save and carry forward elements basic to myths in transition.

By the time I got back to the panhandle, to see things for myself, to walk the blackened prairie, talk to devastated farmers and ranchers, wildlife managers, look for the creatures who, unseen by day, had always left their tracks by night, I wondered additionally about wildfires of an earlier period before the small farms and ranches, the human settlement. Prairie fires were regarded as natural, as inevitable. But that was before there was a built prairie.

One of the most shocking realities of the panhandle fires, repeated over and over, was the fright of the cattle and horses. Early speculation was that muscles remember, that instinctively all animals, wild and domesticated, would try to escape as their ancestors had. They would run. Yes, some of the horses and cattle ran; yes, their owners cut fences, opened gates, tried to move them by horse-back, truck, ATV, even by chasing on foot behind them. But there were numerous accounts of the ultimate confusion of these animals, how they froze fearfully in the face of fire, not knowing what to do, perhaps domesticated to a degree by our "care," by the habit of cor-ral, lot, fenced pasture that bound them.

One of the accounts in the immediate aftermath of the fire brought this fact painfully home. A couple from Panhandle, Texas, sixty miles east of Amarillo, had battled the unrelenting 60 mph wind and fire around their house and barns. They poured water, tossed shovels of dirt on orange, glowing pieces of wood that came within ten feet of their house. The house saved, the barn partially destroyed, the wife, Kathy, walked down to the corrals to look for the cats that had lived there and for various livestock including the horses on the place. She came back in tears.

What she found was a young horse, still alive after the fire storms, in the corner of what remained of the barn. Apparently, the traumatized colt stood bolt still as the fire nearly engulfed him and indeed burned his face and body. He still stood but with an awful shaking. Seeing his owner, he managed a few more moments until—instinctively knowing he had to stand to live—he collapsed, lay on his side, eventually died.

Of course, the major concern (if one followed the front-page news in the Amarillo *Globe-Times*, which ran fire stories daily in March, even after the fire's containment) was the loss of human lives and property. Four people dead, 350,000 miles of fencing and farm structures damaged or destroyed, and about 960,000 acres scorched. The cost of replacing a mile of fence is five thousand dollars. Loss of livestock settled into about the five thousand range rather than the originally estimated ten thousand. But the story of the colt—fixed in his suffering, his fright, his entrapment—stuck. Someone said that with so much lost—the atmosphere still filled by the gray of floating ashes—only something called spirit remained.

Back down in the Chihuahuan Desert, where I work at the local uni-versity, you live with aridity, an average humidity of six percent, annual rainfall six inches—no fire, but at least considerable heat, especially in the summers. Instead of fire, a flood hit El Paso, dumping six inches of rain in two hours, following considerable moisture amounts in the previous days, eventually causing a hundred million dollars in damage and ravaging three hundred homes. At my condominium, my neighbor's silver-gray VW slipped off into an arroyo drainage area that rushed "like Niagara." It was discovered later that the city had not kept the arroyos clear of debris. Rocks and trash carried by the rushing flood undermined the stone and concrete sides, the parking lot caving into the drainage area. The VW slipped in, nose down, filling so completely with the accumulating rocks and trash that only a work crew with picks and axes could get it out weeks after the storm.

But out in the surrounding desert, in fact in town along the slopes of the Franklin Mountains, and then up and down I-25 north all the way to Albuquerque, the desert bloomed. What should have been the normal summer's heat-stressed plants bloomed again, as in spring. Local botanists, experts in desert flora, witnessed in amazement the blooming of species not seen in a hundred years. For once this desert, a portion identified on maps as the Jornado de Muerto, now appeared to be a sea of grass.

My students and I stand in one of the arroyo washes after this storm, hands sheltering our eyes against the sun, some of us guarded by our black wrap-around sunglasses. Scott Cutler, a geologist and head of University of Texas at El Paso's Centennial Museum, holds up a photograph of the area from the Franklin Mountains to the Rio Grande basin showing the arroyo where we stand. "We are here," he says, pointing to the blue-green streaked section of the inkjet photo. I immediately feel slightly out of body, seeing where we are in the photograph, yet simultaneously standing in the actual arroyo, looking up to where it runs to the Franklin peaks a couple of miles away. "It's hard to appreciate what is before us," he continues. "Like this rock for instance." (He bends to collect a seemingly nondescript white, oblong rock, just palm size.) "Look at how it is smooth on all sides, obviously a rock washed from the flutes on the sides of the Franklin mountain and down this arroyo." He had been talking to my students about the arroyo system in El Paso, some 250 arroyos, which came to everyone's attention during the recent flood.

But what Scott said next surprised everyone. Sure the mountain had loosed its elements, releasing stones that covered this arroyo. They were everywhere; in fact, the arroyo itself was defined by thousands of fist-sized stones upon which we stood.

"It's hard for us humans to get our minds around the timeline of a rock," he said. "This one, for instance, is probably about thirty million years old, and it took some of that time for it to get down the mountain to where we stand. So we, with maybe a life expectancy of eighty years, are standing among stones whose movement took that long to get them to this place in the arroyo." I understood at that moment the nature of my odd feeling—what it meant to be in a space between what something is and what it is becoming. And how this space, like the effect of time in Scott's photo, makes us aware that place—the mountains unfluting themselves—is ever-changing.

I thought then of an earlier time in my life when I had lived in another desert, the high desert near Albuquerque, New Mexico. Working as executive director for the National Endowment for the Humanities, the state council for programming in the humanities, I enjoyed particularly the guidance of three Native Americans, two Pueblo men and a Navajo, who were instrumental in our contribution to a funding project in Santa Fe at a local seed bank. The project undertook to provide nonhybridized native corn seeds from Tesuque Pueblo north of Santa Fe to parts of famine- and drought-beset Ethiopia. The idea was that, unlike the hybridized seeds provided in some relief efforts, these were sustainable. The native seeds had a chance to come up year after year. The ambitious project entailed air-dropping the color-coded seeds along with a tiny map-like illustration that showed how to plant them. It seemed at once both a giant project and a small one. The idea of distributing seeds across the world, and in a country historically separated by formidable mountain ranges, river gorges, and desert, was daunting. The "humanities" part of the project had to do with the role of native seeds in cultural sustainability and how these could be shared with other desert dwellers on the other side of the globe.

Tesuque, surrounded by Santa Fe development, had until recently ceased to have its yearly corn dance. The reason: the pueblo had stopped growing corn. Unlike other more distant pueblos,

Tesuque felt the manpower drain from the proximity of the pueblo to the nonreservation city. People left. Or they worked day jobs and sporadically returned home. Particularly the passing of traditions to the young had been affected when the ceremonies of planting, harvesting were lost. To help, Hopi loaned Tesuque some of their own reserve corn seeds. Some of the corn given to Tesuque possibly were "ancient" seeds saved in storage jars for exceedingly dry seasons. With the planting of this corn at Tesuque came harvests and the return ceremonial dances. From these corn harvests, Tesuque donated seeds for relief in Ethiopia. I liked to think of the corn-filled packets sifting down from the aerial drops, distributing New World corn to the oldest cradle of mankind. If I had wondered through the years of moving around what it meant to return to landscape, now I asked what it meant for the landscape to return to us.

Back home in Vega in the summer, without rain for almost nine months, including the period of the fires in March, the town and Oldham County were recommending fire ditches around houses, but also entire pastures. I walked in a pasture about ten miles south of Armitage Farms, witnessing a specter sight. In the midst of the charred, blackened prairie were green cholla cacti still standing. How had the fire swept the ground around those cacti without taking them down? It could have been the height of the grass but also the moisture, the water content inside the cactus, that prevented them from catching fire.

Like everyone else, I opted for the fire lanes. Prairie left somehow unscathed was now systematically graded up—a lane about twelve feet across—the tractor blade scraping the natural turf down to the hardpan. The experience was visceral for me. I could feel the rip like flesh. A kind of wound, this loss of habitat. I was reminded of how I feel when I pass the new developments, the "farmettes" going up along frontage roads west of Amarillo as the city sprawls. Native soil is scraped off, square acreage laid out, two-story houses (mostly), large and lacking any environmental sense or historical connection to their landscape, quickly built. All finished out with new Midwest, thirsty sod. The new prairie ideal. The domestication of the short-grass prairie. I felt that same tear as the soil, house to house for the fire lanes, was strafed aside.

West of these farmettes, a new wind energy field is going up, stretching into Oldham County. The company grades miles and miles of Canadian escarpment into the necessary large network of roads. All summer, I note the trucks hauling water up and down the connecting county road for the road building in a region known for its water shortage. East of Vega, near Pantex, the Department of Energy plutonium dismantling facility, I hear that horny toads are fitted with small backpacks so they can be scientifically tracked to see if any potential pollution or habitat disruption at the site impacts their community. North, some ranches are sold to owners who develop them as "strip mines," as huge caliche and sand and gravel pits take down the mesas. South, there is still land earmarked in the federal government DOE's records for the building, possibly in the future, of a high-level nuclear waste dump site.

But for now we enjoy something very strange that happened this fall. Possibly it is an aspect of global warming, like the floods, the fires, the droughts. A six-inch rain fell in two days on the blackened and blanched burnt earth in the eastern panhandle. A little more than that fell in the western panhandle. It seemed that almost overnight a consistent tall prairie grass—black grama—covered everything. This grass heads in a horizontal flag of darker seeds from the vertical parent stalk. From a distance, the undulation is a green topped with what looks like a faint but uniform magenta, thus a rich-looking carpet close to the ground with softly moving lavender flags. The cattleman who leases our grassland held off for a month from putting his cattle back on the place because he didn't want to disturb the astounding beauty. Maybe part of the reluctance was the unusualness of this much grass, this single variety dominating, this uniformity of beauty that suggests that earlier epithet: the sea of grass. There was a desire not to break it, interrupt it. While mowers whirled in town to tidy up yards gone ragged, out on the prairie people waited. Sometimes muscles—seeds, stones, too—remember.

four mountains

KURT CASWELL

And so that morning of June 27, 2007, in heavy rain and fog, I thought I might climb Mount Snowdon alone, the highest mountain in Wales. The waitress at Pete's Eats in Llanberis, where I breakfasted on a monster omelet, open faced, with chips, told me only professionals climb Snowdon in this kind of weather. And a kind old woman at a shop where I bought fruit, cheese, and bread for the trail said, "What? You're going up Snowdon? In this weather?" We looked out together at the rain slashing sideways at the windows.

"Why? Don't people climb Snowdon in this weather?" I asked.

"Only if they're mad."

Therefore, I stepped out the door, squared off with the rain, and up I went, up the Llanberis Path, the most direct, least technical of the several routes to the summit.

Wordsworth climbed this mountain too, and wrote an account in his epic poem *The Prelude*. He went at night with a companion, and a shepherd as his guide, intent on seeing the sunrise from the summit. If I understand his poem, Wordsworth makes an astonishing discovery on that ascent. He comes to this great truth: "the highest

bliss / That flesh can know . . ." is "To hold fit converse with the
spiritual world." Perhaps you're thinking this isn't news at all, but
there is a great difference in the wisdom that comes by experience,
and the wisdom that comes by way of musty books. To know, as others have said, you must make the journey yourself. The climb
becomes a pilgrimage for Wordsworth, wherein he works out a kind
of thesis for his life. The moment of discovery, he relates, "fell like a
flash" before him. He looked up into the night sky to find "the Moon
hung naked in a firmament / Of azure without cloud, and at [his]
feet / Rested a silent sea of hoary mist." It's a beautiful moment, a
beautiful passage, and upon reading it, any wistful wanderer like
myself cannot but ask: if it happened for Wordsworth on this sacred
mountain, why can't it happen for me?

But I had come to the UK for more practical reasons: (1) to
attend a writers' conference at Bangor University; (2) to travel with
an old friend from my native Oregon; and (3) for sheep. I know. I
know. There are all the various jokes and whatnot—but for me,
sheep are serious business. I had spent some time traveling with
shepherds in Idaho intent on writing about their lives, and so I
thought the next step in my inquiry was to explore the pastoral
landscapes of Great Britain. I had financial support too, a grant
from Texas Tech University where I teach. If I had any sense at all, I
would have roused to this good fortune. Isn't it every writer's dream
to be handed a substantial budget and told: "Go find something to
write about." But truth is I was wracked with guilt. What did I mean
by "explore"? Where was my "inquiry" headed? Why sheep, for
god's sake? Quite possibly nothing at all would emerge from my
journey, and then I'd have to answer to the State of Texas for my
irresponsible behavior. I was rather used to failure, but so far I had
mostly done it with my own money.

I rounded an elbow on the Llanberis Path and passed a country
house at the foot of the mountain. Here I came to a sign that told me
not to expect toilets, shelter, or a café at the summit, luxuries I had
no reason to expect until I learned I could not expect them. A little
farther on, another sign appeared that read: "This is sheep country.
Keep your dog on a lead." Perhaps the State of Texas would get good

value for its money after all. Thus emboldened, like Wordsworth "I panted up / With eager pace, and no less eager thoughts," the black slugs, hideous and strange, making a gastropodinal minefield in front of me. Incidentally, it turns out that black slugs are not only black, but various shades of that color, which I understand to mean gray, and they can also be white. If you want to cull the population in your garden, the two best methods are, according to my source, dousing them with salt, or boiling them in a saucepan on your kitchen stove.

The rain let up, and I felt like the day might go my way. I picked up the pace and shed my Gortex rain shell, strapping it happily to my Osprey daypack. My boots were comfortable, and so far dry, and I could see ahead that I was gaining on two figures in the distance. I felt hale and fit as I overtook them, two young women in sporty outdoor apparel. I passed on the left and said "Good morning," to which they enthusiastically offered the same. I suppose I might have slowed and walked with them, but did I want company on my climb? Not really. At least I didn't think I did. I pressed onward and up, passing a few scattered sheep, toward the heavy cloud bank settled in over the mountain. A huge boulder appeared out in front of me. My map told the story of a local legend: if you spend the night near the boulder you will experience a transformation—you wake up either a poet or a lunatic.

Thinking it better to avoid both, I developed a steady cadence as I humped up the mountain, and soon became so preoccupied in my mind thinking god knows what that I didn't notice the railroad tracks along the route until I passed under them, and then farther on, under them again, where at last I reached the ceiling of the sky. Apparently people don't always climb this mountain, but instead hop the train to the summit. I couldn't imagine a Wordsworthian epiphany arising out of that kind of voluptuousness, but here, as I paused beneath the stone overpass, it began to rain again, and I wondered if the train wouldn't happen by and stop for me. The temperature fell and the wind burned my exposed ears. Visibility was only fifty feet, perhaps even thirty, here in the misty clouds. What if in my blindness I walked off the western face and plunged to my gory death? Unlikely, and yet I thought about turning back. Then I thought about thinking about turning back: Would I think about turning back if I were climbing with my old friend? No. We'd press on through the storm. I put on my toboggan, then my rain shell, and pulled the Gortex hood over my head.

I had not felt lonely until now, and when it came it surprised me. I was alone on the back of the greatest mountain in Wales suffering impossible weather, and no one in the world really knew where I was. A million miles from home, I was hungry and tired and emotionally bereft. Because no one knew me, and there was no one here to know me, I thought I could be anyone in anywhen, and oddly the idea of wandering out of my old life made me happy. I wasn't happy exactly, but rather happy that I was lonely. I thought of Basho and the three conditions for his haiku: *sabi*, or loneliness, *shiori*, or tenderness, and *hosomi*, or slenderness. I thought maybe I had them all, and when I reached the summit, I hoped to find waiting for me a sort of grail, an answer to a question I had not asked. Who could accomplish such a knight's errand but me? And Wordsworth, of course.

Then I heard voices. Lots of voices. Were they the songs of guiding angels descending with the rain? No, for out of the mist came a colorful band of several dozen schoolchildren, laughing and shouting and splashing in the rain. A couple of smiling teachers brought up the rear. "Cheers," one of them said, as they passed on by. So much for heroics. I ate six Fig Newtons, then stepped out into the rain and muscled up the way. I could hardly see anything at all, but I found that as I walked deeper into the mist, a little more of the trail ahead was revealed to me, and in this way I reached the top of the mountain.

At the summit stone I now understood the sign below announcing that there were no services at the top. Not because there were no services at the top, but because the services at the top were under renovation. A dozen men scurried about concrete foundations, and several excavators tore into the mountain's skin making a horrendous racket. I stood there a moment in the sharp wind, the surrounding peaks of Snowdonia obscured from my view, and noted how utterly anticlimactic. I wondered if I would have found the summit more enchanting had I climbed the mountain with my friend. As it was, alone and battered by the bitter wind, the universal mystery did not reveal itself to me the way it had for Wordsworth, and I imagined no length of waiting around would change this fact. What was the problem, anyway? Were these not conditions ripe for a miracle? Were such miracles even possible? Here in the yeasty heights, I had to come face to face with the possibility that the great poet was full of shit. Then a thought rose up in me: If not here, why not there, why not climb another great mountain with my old friend when he arrived in Dublin? What is the highest mountain in Ireland, anyway? In fact, why not climb all the greatest mountains in the UK, in England, Scotland, Ireland, and Wales? Perhaps Wordsworth had not led me astray after all. I offered the summit a final nod, knowing I'd likely never return, and started back down the mountain.

MOUNT CARRANTUOHIL, IRELAND (1,039 METERS/3,409 FEET)

Basho traveled with a companion, Sora. Samuel Johnson explored the Hebrides with James Boswell. Bruce Chatwin claimed to travel alone, but he lied—he almost always went with a friend. Peter Matthiessen accompanied George Schaller into the Himalayas. And of course Wordsworth and Coleridge made regular walking tours in the Lake District. This tradition of traveling with a companion inspired me, and it was in Matthiessen's book, *The Snow Leopard*, that I read: "The Roshi was pleased that there would be but two of us—this seemed to him a condition of true pilgrimage." If making a solitary ascent of Snowdon was to bear me no fruit, perhaps hill walking with a friend would. Besides, I was tired of traveling alone and tired of being lonely. To my good fortune, my old friend Scott Dewing had agreed to meet me in Dublin.

Scott and I had grown up together, passing through those affected high school years and on through college. It was a kind of miracle—more so than Wordsworth's inspiration in the face of natural beauty—that after twenty-three years my friendship with Scott was still intact. No. Better than intact. It was flourishing, which was far more than I could say for the numerous friends whose lives I had

passed in and out of over the years. Certainly we had our differences. Scott was married with two daughters; I was married and now
wasn't (we were each best man at the other's wedding). Scott had
put on fifty unnecessary pounds and lost his hair; I had grown my
hair long and kept fairly fit. Scott had moved from northwest Oregon to southwest Oregon, with a few flights into the foreign; I had
moved from northwest Oregon to almost every state in the west, and
hit twenty-four countries along the way. I admired his steadiness;
he admired my wanderlust. I sometimes longed for his family life;
he sometimes longed for my solitude. He could still kick my ass, but
I was sure I could outrun him. Yet we both still loved books and
good writing, outdoor and indoor adventures, and long walks on the
beach. Even as months, sometimes years, passed between visits, we
always seemed to pick up where we left off. After high school, Scott
and I had planned to make a journey together through Peru, but college and lovers and making a living took precedent, and we left that
dream behind. Now at long last, such a journey was imminent. I
took this as a sign of good fortune, and after a long day of wandering
Dublin in the rain, Scott and I boarded the train for Killarney Town
to climb Carrantuohil, the highest peak in Ireland.

From Cronin's Yard, the path leads up the Gaddagh River to the
Devil's Ladder, a steep scree-filled gully eroded by the thousands of
hill walkers who make this trek each year. The sun broke through
the clouds, as Scott and I walked through Hag's Glen and between
the brilliant waters of Lough Callee and Lough Gouragh. We felt
good and talked about old times, the mountain sheep grazing the
green green grass.

At the Ladder, I pulled easily away from Scott, scrambling over
huge boulders, slick in the rain, as we rose up dramatically off the
valley floor. I was passing other hill walkers with ease, and I felt fit
and fast and wanted to go faster. Instead, I stopped shy of halfway to
wait for my companion. Twenty years ago, Scott and I were fairly
competitive, and a situation like this would usually awaken his
anger. He'd fume and sputter to catch up to me, throw his pack
down where I waited, and curse the weather, or the terrain, or his
shoes. He wasn't used to losing. He was bigger, stronger, and faster

than me, but over the long haul, I usually beat him. Now it mattered not at all. Scott's life was full and complete, and he devoted himself daily to his family and his work as a teacher and computer administrator. As I was single again, I filled some of my idle hours with running and cycling and wandering just to stave off loneliness. My fitness wasn't a sign of anything, really, except time spent alone.

"How you feelin' man?" Scott said. He put his big hand on my shoulder.

"I'm feelin' great," I said. "You?"

"Haven't felt this good in years. Look at that! Awe, man," he said.

We looked back down the Ladder where the green valley drew a line to the horizon. This would likely be the only grand view we'd get, as the top of Carrantuohil was nearly always occluded by heavy clouds and mist.

"Don't feel like you have to wait on me," Scott said. "I'll make my way up at my own pace."

"No, man," I said. "Let's walk it together."

The plot to climb the four highest mountains in England, Scotland, Ireland, and Wales rose out of our friendship and out of our search for a purpose. I had thought to climb Snowdon in Wales and Scafell Pike in England because these were the mountains of the great pastoral poets Wordsworth and Coleridge, but to climb them all, and climb them together, that came out of some deeper need to get things done. Much of my friendship with Scott revolved around getting things done—we skied the closed Forest Service roads deep into the Cascades; we trained for and completed a triathlon at age sixteen; we created a course for ourselves in Egyptology when our high school failed to inspire; we ran the steep, winding trail to the top of 620-foot Multnomah Falls, the second highest waterfall in the USA; we paddled canoes up and down the great Columbia. Some of this was youthful exuberance, but we also made a concerted effort to lead each other forward, to imagine heroic labors because there seemed to be no one to imagine them for us. It was quite by accident when one day we realized that those labors had made us the best of friends. Now here we were again, two decades later, up to our old tricks.

It started to rain, not much, but enough so that we both put on our rain gear. We climbed and rested and talked all the way to

Christ's Saddle, and then on up to the great iron cross on the summit. It was busy at the top, hill walkers everywhere talking and eating and laughing. Scott asked the fellow next to us if he would take our picture together near the cross. As it was for me on Snowdon, we couldn't see a thing through the clouds. We found a rock shelter safe from the wind, and spread out our lunch: cheese and hard salami, bread, fruit, and canned oysters. Aristotle is no friend of mine, but I do know that in his *Nicomachean Ethics* he devotes a number of pages to friendship, stating that "friends are the only refuge," and that "without friends no one would choose to live." I certainly felt that now, as here on Carrantuohil I wasn't anticipating the revelation of the universal mystery, but rather the long, slow hike down engaged in conversation with my old friend, and later, gorging on meat and Guinness at a Killarney pub. A much better option than epiphany. I reached for the oysters then, and a ray of sunlight broke over my hand. Blue sky cracked the mountain peak as the clouds parted and rolled down into the valley. The bustle at the summit went still, and everyone everywhere stood up. There was Ireland! The Slieve Mish Mountains on the Dingle Peninsula. The Galty Mountains to the east in Tipperary. Kenmare Bay to the southwest, and Inch and Rossbeigh Strand to the northwest. Cameras buzzed and snapped, but Scott and I just stood there looking out. This is a scene for poets, I thought, and to be shared among friends.

Later, showered and happy and empty, Scott and I asked the slender beauty at the desk of Neptune's Hostel where we might find a good meal and a good beer.

"The Laurels," she said. "That's the place you want."

"How do we get there?" Scott asked.

"All right, then," she said. "You go out onto the front street there, that's New Street. Take a left. Then right on High Street. You can't miss it." Then she paused as if channeling the muse. "It will just hit you," she said, "like fate."

BEN NEVIS, SCOTLAND (1,344 METERS/4,409 FEET)

In Fort William, over wild boar burgers and Guinness at the Grog & Gruel, I couldn't think of anything else to complain about so I complained about my good fortune.

"I don't know. Is this research?" I said. "I mean, how can I spend this grant money on climbing these mountains?"

"Dude," Scott said. "This is what you do. Would you rather be in a library somewhere reading some archive?"

"No way."

"See, you gotta let that go. You're collecting data. It's just that your data is experience."

"Yeah, yeah, I know," I said. "But will the university president buy that? I mean I'm enjoying this. I can't imagine doing anything else right now. Administrations don't cotton to fun."

"Christ," Scott said. "This is the best money the State of Texas has ever spent. Look at it this way—you're supposed to be learning right? Gaining knowledge and using that knowledge to write and teach?"

"Right."

"So, experience as data—at least in my view—leaps over the whole tedious stage called 'research' and directly to knowledge. You don't have to research anything. Experience is knowledge. That's the difference between research in the humanities and research in the sciences. Your school is getting good value for its money, much better value than a scientist who goes on and on spending money for decades, data set after data set only to conclude that people have sex because they're attracted to each other."

"Right, but—"

"No buts, man," Scott said. "You could write a whole fuckin' paper on this difference, don't you think? But who would want to. It'd be called something like"—and with that, he worked out a proper title to appease my overindulgent guilt—"Differential Data Gathering Methodologies between the Sciences and the Humanities, Or, How to Use Your Research Funding to Vacation in Europe."

"That's genius," I said. "That ought to do it."

"Right," he said. "Plus you went to that conference, read your work, made contacts, and gave your school a good name."

"Yeah."

"And then you'll use these experiences to write your shepherd book."

"True."

"And you'll share this journey with your students, not to mention

your colleagues, who always benefit when their teachers actually live
a life, rather than sit home and watch reality TV."

"Indeed," I said.

"And other pieces will come out of it, too. I mean, maybe you'll
write about this."

"Maybe," I said.

"So give it a rest," he said. "Plus, look at it this way: the grant
won't even pay for beer, right? So here you are again spending your
own damn money to bring all this knowledge back to your school. I
find that almost criminal."

Ben Nevis, the highest peak in Scotland, and in the UK, was just
out our door from the Calluna Hostel. After a night of reading melo-
dramatic poetry about the mountain—

Oh! for a sight of Ben Nevis!
Methinks I see him now,
As the morning sunlight crimsons
The snow-wreath on his brow . . .

—followed by a little Burns and Sir Walter Scott, then a three-hour
commitment to Mel Gibson's *Braveheart* (we were bent on Scottish
immersion after all), we walked the several kilometers to the trail-
head, and started up toward the Red Burn. We'd come to learn that a
popular challenge in the UK was to climb Snowdon, Ben Nevis, and
England's Scafell Pike all within twenty-four hours—I boasted that I
would climb all of them too, Carrantuohil included, in twenty-four
days.

We came up out of the alder and Scots pine, the violets,
heathers, and primrose at the bottom of the glen, and into deer
grass, bog asphodel, butterworts, and sundews at Halfway Lochan.
The mountain, as usual, was shrouded in mist. Likely all we would
see at the summit were other people, hundreds of people streaming
up the mountain track. (About a hundred thousand people reach the
summit each year.) And sheep, which were everywhere on the green
hillsides. I stopped often to snap photographs.

"More pictures of sheep, huh?" Scott said. "That'll show those
bastards."

Few friendships weather the great, ordinary life transitions:

youth to adulthood, single life to married life, student-idealist to pragmatic citizen. How ours did, I'll never know. Perhaps it was the way in which Scott and I helped raise each other. We both had powerful, emotionally distant fathers who instructed primarily by way of pragmatism and criticism. My father's style was to put me in an oar boat on a big western river and push me off into the swirling current. "Don't hit any rocks," he'd call after me. "I paid good money for that boat." That was one way, and a pretty good one too, but it didn't cover all the ground. Scott had an older brother, but they weren't so close in those days, and I had grown up with two sisters. There were those hallmarks of western male society—athletics, the frat house, the military—but they were either insufficient, or we skipped them altogether. So there were holes in our journey to manhood, and we each turned to the other to fill them.

A boy becomes a man only "through ritual and effort—only through the 'active intervention of older men,'" writes Robert Bly in *Iron John*. He cannot make the transition from the care and protection of women (his mother, primarily) to the society of men (his father, primarily) without help. And he requires the help of older men. "Having no soul union with other men can be the most damaging wound of all," asserts Bly. Back in the day, the men would enter the mother's house with spears, snatch up the boy, and take him by force to the edge of the village. There the boy would be instructed by other initiated men, his father among them, and upon returning home, he would indeed be a man with a man's responsibilities. Without this kind of ceremony, and without such strong, emotionally open older men to show the way, a son will have what Bly calls "father hunger all his life." I have felt this father hunger, and felt it most deeply when Scott and I were rounding out our high school years. It's not that our fathers did nothing, or tried not at all, but that they didn't go far enough. At the threshold of manhood, it was Scott who was there for me, just as I was there for him.

When Scott and I were sixteen, my father suggested, in the way that he did, that we take the drift boat and run the upper John Day River to Clarno. Perhaps he knew what he was doing after all, kicking us out of the house to work off a little baby fat. Scott and I drove out to eastern Oregon with food and gear for three days, along with a little contraband: a gallon of cheap wine, a half case of beer, a fifth of Jack Daniels. That first night on the river, after having run several small class II rapids and endured the cold fall winds and rain, we grilled elk burgers on the fire and topped our glasses with JD. The sky cleared for just that night, and standing there under the simple stars, the hunger in my belly near insatiable, we raised a toast to brotherhood. Though I recognize it only now, these many years later, it was that moment that stands as my initiation ceremony, and it was Scott who was there to share it with me.

At a thousand feet higher than all other mountains in the United Kingdom, our climb up Ben Nevis didn't want to end. We climbed, up and up, crossing a snow field near the summit. Soon we could see a series of humps on the arc of the mountain's back, humps that were the many rock shelters at trail's end. Once again, as if the landlord was looking out for us, the clouds broke and the sun shone through. We walked the final steps bathed in light, and as it was so, we had no old complaints, no new desires.

SCAFELL PIKE, ENGLAND (978 METERS/3,209 FEET)

Wordsworth and Coleridge were as brothers for a time, and they famously lived in proximity in England's Lake District, composing their greatest poems with the other's favor and guidance. Dorothy was there too, Wordsworth's beloved sister, and the three walked miles and miles together through the hills and glens. The height of their friendship was also the height of their poetic industry. Coleridge wrote "The Rime of the Ancyent Marinere," and Wordsworth was already at work on the poem that became his epic, *The Prelude*. They published a volume together, *Lyrical Ballads*, which was largely a failure then, but a staple of Romantic poetry now. On a walk to Keswick, near England's highest mountain, Scafell Pike, Coleridge exclaimed, in typical Romantic bombast:

> O my God! and the Black Crags close under the snowy mountains, whose snows were pinkish with the setting sun and the reflections from the sandy rich Clouds that floated over some and rested upon others! It was to me a vision of fair Country.

I had never been to the Lake District, and so anticipated fair country as well, not to mention—O my God!—my deepest immersion yet in all things pastoral, all things Romantic, all things sheep. Well, not *all* things sheep.

After a few nights in Edinburgh, where Scott and I explored the pastoral paintings in the National Gallery; the Writers' Museum (devoted to Burns, Scott, and Stevenson); the work of that intrepid walker, Richard Long, at the National Gallery of Modern Art; and where a drunk witch named Sabrina crawled up into my bunk at the Backpackers Hostel and whispered, "I just wanna cuddle," we struck south for Wordsworth-land to climb Scafell Pike, the last mountain on the list. Scott was nearing the end of his journey, while I would travel on for several more weeks. My indemnity had become so dependent on my companion I could hardly imagine what I'd do after he left.

It was raining, of course, when in Grasmere Scott and I boarded a bus for Keswick, then on to Seathwaite, which was not a town, but rather the end of the road. We passed through the gates of a sheep outfit, where the shepherds kicked their dogs and beat the ewes into a pen, to find unfolding before us a system of trails ascending the hoary crags. We walked easily and steadily in the light rain, up Grains Gill and along Seathwaite Fell. Soon we would make a turn up Ruddy Gill, and then onto the Esk Hause trail to the summit. Though Scafell Pike was the lowest of the four mountains, the climb challenged us more with trails running every direction through the wilds, and the rough-going over misty boulder fields.

Wordsworth had his Mount Snowdon, but it was Coleridge who scrambled up Scafell, not the mountain we were climbing, but the one next to it with nearly the same name. Some think of Scafell and Scafell Pike as the same mountain, but each has a distinct summit, the latter fourteen meters higher. At the top of Scafell, Coleridge, never without pen and ink, worked on a letter to his beloved Sara Hutchinson. Sara was the sister of Wordsworth's wife, Mary, and not to be confused with Coleridge's wife, also named Sara. That done, Coleridge thought he could see a route to the summit of Scafell Pike (which apparently he thought was Bowfell farther to the east), the mountain local shepherds believed the highest in the land. He had

no map, no compass, no guide or guidebook. He relied only on his
poetic sense. The going was hard, and he found the ridge between
the two mountains too much for him. Abandoning Scafell Pike, he
started back down, dropping over vertical ledges onto narrow
shelves of rock. He passed the carcass of a sheep, "quite rotten,"
which had fallen to its death. Not altogether a good sign. Soon he
reached an impossible ledge, impossible for him anyway, and there
he was, cragfast—he could neither go up nor down. "My limbs were
all a tremble—," he wrote later to Sara Hutchinson:

> I lay upon my Back to rest myself, and was beginning according
> to my Custom, to laugh at myself for a Madman, when the sight
> of the Crags above me on each side, and the impetuous Clouds
> just over them, posting so luridly and so rapidly northward,
> overawed me. I lay in a state of almost prophetic Trance and
> Delight—

Somehow, perhaps with Providence on his side, he discovered a
great crack (known today as Fat Man's Agony), which he thought
might just be the only way down. He moved his rucksack to his side,
and down he went stemming his way to the bottom. Clouds closed in
around him, and the rain fell. He hustled down the mountain
toward Eskdale where he took shelter from the storm in a sheepfold.
From the enthusiasm in his notebook and letters, one must conclude this treacherous climb was the highlight of his 1802 solo tour
of the Lakes.

Scott and I crossed over the murmuring brook of Grains Gill,
where we paused on the footbridge for photos. I carried in my pack
a few bars of the famed Kendal mint cake, a soft, sugary energy bar,
which Hillary and Norgay took to the summit of Everest. I broke one
open and we shared it out. From here we could see a good way in
both directions—down the gill, and up into where we were going.
The rain came on, and we took the time to put on our rain gear. A
little farther up the trail, we stopped again and took off our rain
gear—this time for the last time. Though clouds hung heavy over the
mountain peaks, it wouldn't rain again for a couple days. Up we
climbed into the clouds where the moist air wetted our hair and

clothes. Sun fell across the broad green backs of the hills in patches, and I wondered if I'd ever seen anything so beautiful. I thought probably I had.

We crossed a great boulder field where the sheep would not go, skipping from stone to stone in our boots. At the top of Broad Crag we descended, down onto the tongue between them, the crag and mighty Scafell Pike. So here it was, our final ascent. We noticed a few other climbers in bright colors among the rocks winding slowly up the mountain, but compared to Ben Nevis and Carrantuohil, we had the place mostly to ourselves. I broke off a couple more pieces of mint cake, and with that cool, sweet courage we climbed to the top. There wasn't much to it really, at least from this side, and we met with no dastardly threat to our health or heels. The mist and heavy clouds allowed us no grand view across the Lake District, so we found a proper seat among the boulders to spread our lunch.

I wondered if, like Coleridge after listening to Wordsworth read from his great epic, I might not be overwhelmed at this juncture, at the completion of this journey with my old friend, by "thoughts all too deep for words!—," and then might I fall delicately into a reverie, part trance and part delight. But no—for thence erupted from my lips, without my consent, a string of hopeful words:

"You gonna eat that?" I asked, indicating the last bit of hard salami.

"Nope," Scott said.

And that was it; there was nothing more, but the shorter, faster grind back down the mountain, a happy, sunny ride through the countryside on the second level of an open-air bus, and in the evening, food and beer without end.

In Ambleside, the morning of Scott's departure, we walked together from the big hostel on the lake to the bus stop. We had hardly slept at all, as the hostel was overrun with a belligerent rugby team, shouting drunken obscenities and vomiting in the hallways. Scott would take the early bus to Windermere, and then catch the train south to London. I felt a terrible anxiety welling within, and I didn't think it was lack of sleep. Before Scott's arrival, I had emboldened myself to travel alone (not the first time, certainly), and made my way through Wales and up Mount Snowdon. But something in me had shifted, and I was flooded now with questions. What in god's name would I do with myself after Scott's departure? When would we see each other again? Would we ever make another journey? What if one of us kicked off without warning and this was really, really the end? What does one say in a moment of such finality? I still had a couple weeks to travel before I went home, and who now would I talk to over good food and beer? Who would help me plan the route, and take up the idle hours of the day? Who would hold my confidence, my hesitations, my deep expostulations, and return them with a generous reply? Who would watch my stuff on the train when I got up to take a piss? We had grown together across these mountaintops—I could feel it—and now this sudden separation knocked about my heart. I was struck by a sense of fear and emptiness. I wanted to express my brotherly love, to say something lasting and profound that we'd never forget. The bus pulled in, just like that, and in that hurried way that people take their leave when consumed with the details of schedules and connections, we shook hands and he was gone.

What else could I do but go a-walking. In the wake of my great friend, I took up my pack, provisioned just so with water and mint cake, and made a turn through town and out toward Lily Tarn. I followed trails I did not know, out beyond Ivy Crag and Loughrigg Fell, walking, walking, walking to shrug off my loneliness. I passed Rydal Cave and Rydal Water until I arrived at the Wordsworths' fond old home, the house and beautiful gardens, the poet's library and study, then through the trees and back around toward Ambleside, I wandered. Posting rapidly over those footpaths, the Lake District felt more alien to me than ever, more so even than the first day when Scott and I arrived. I hardly recognized myself or anything at all: no bird, no flower, no tree, no face looked to me familiar. Where were the birds I knew, the great falcons and hawks of my native land, the western meadowlark and mountain bluebird, the blue heron and sandhill crane? Where the Douglas fir and rhododendron, vine and bigleaf maple, the wild blueberries, serviceberries, Oregon grape, and trillium? There were no beaver or black bear, no elk or mule deer or coyote. I was utterly lost and bereft and the sun was falling in its arc. Like Basho I wanted to sit down on my hat and weep to forget all time, but I steeled my constitution against it and so, pressed on. I wandered, and wandered lonely as a cloud through the fields and fells near Ambleside, until, later, at the threshold of the dining room, a radiant Taiwanese approached me with her three friends. She said, in perfect British English, "Hello. I'm Xiaolin. Won't you come out for a walk?"

contributors

SHELLEY ARMITAGE is professor of English at the University of Texas at El Paso where she teaches literature, interdisciplinary studies, environmental writing, and cultural studies, and held the Dorrance D. Roderick Professorship. She has been a Fulbright scholar in Portugal, Finland, and Hungary, and in Poland as American Literature and Culture Chair. She currently serves on a Fulbright selection committee and is a board member of the Swann Foundation of the Library of Congress. Author of eight books and numerous scholarly articles and essays, her awards include a *New York Times* Notable Book, the Eudora Welty Prize, the Emily Toth Award, and a Border Regional Library Association Southwest Book Award. Other awards include three NEH grants, two Rockefeller grants, and an NEA grant. She was a 2009 resident in creative nonfiction at the Wurlitzer Foundation of Taos where she worked on a memoir about the Canadian River Valley. She spends her summers managing a family farm and grassland near Vega, Texas.

KURT CASWELL is a writer and an assistant professor of creative writing and literature in the Honors College at Texas Tech University. He is a graduate of the Bread Loaf School of English at Middlebury College, and the Bennington Writing Seminars, where he was recipient of the Lucy Grealy Memorial Scholarship. He is the author of two books: *An Inside Passage* (University of Nebraska Press,

2009), which won the 2008 River Teeth Literary Nonfiction Book Prize, and *In the Sun's House: My Year Teaching on the Navajo Reservation* (Trinity University Press, 2009).

Writer, naturalist, and activist SUSAN CERULEAN's nature memoir, *Tracking Desire: A Journey after Swallow-tailed Kites* (University of Georgia Press, 2005) was an *Audubon* magazine Editors' Choice. Cerulean directs the Red Hills Writers Project from her home in northern Florida.

LISA COUTURIER is the author of *The Hopes of Snakes and Other Tales from the Urban Landscape* (Beacon Press, 2005). She is currently at work on a memoir about horses and the Thoroughbred horse racing industry. Her work has appeared in numerous publications, including *Orion*, *Isotope*, and the American Nature Writing series. She lives with her family on an agricultural reserve in Maryland.

MATT DALY is the author of *Wild Nature and the Human Spirit: A Field Guide to Journal Writing in Nature* (Grand Teton Natural History Association, 2004), which includes artwork by Olaus J. Murie. His stories and essays have been published in *Wyoming Fence Lines*, *Stories of the Wild*, and *Ahead of Their Time: Wyoming Voices for Wilderness*. He lives with his wife and son in Jackson Hole, Wyoming, across the Snake River from his childhood home.

Formerly a professional tour guide, field biologist, and door-to-door canvasser, PETER FRIEDERICI is an assistant professor of journalism at Northern Arizona University in Flagstaff. His articles and essays have been published in many periodicals, including *Audubon*, *Orion*, the *Georgia Review*, and *High Country News*. His books include *The Suburban Wild* (University of Georgia Press, 1999) and *Nature's Restoration* (Island Press, 2006), as well as a new, edited collection of oral narratives focusing on environmental change in northern Arizona.

In addition to teaching at Texas State University–San Marcos since 1976, SUSAN HANSON worked for twenty years as a newspaper journalist and has served as lay chaplain for the Episcopal campus ministry at Texas State since 1995. Her work has appeared in *Texas Parks and Wildlife* magazine, *Northern Lights*, *Pilgrimage*, *EarthLight*, the *Nature Writing Newsletter*, and in an anthology, *Getting Over the Color Green*. She is coeditor of *Women Write the Southwest* with Susan Wittig Albert, Jan Epton Seale, and Paula Stallings Yost (University of Texas Press, 2007). Susan's interests include gardening with native plants, traveling, studying the relationship between spirituality and nature, reading mysteries, playing twelve-string guitar, maintaining Web sites, and training her Labrador retriever. She raised one daughter with her husband, Larry.

MARYBETH HOLLEMAN is author of *The Heart of the Sound: An Alaskan Paradise Found and Nearly Lost* and coeditor of *Crosscurrents North: Alaskans on the Environment*. Raised in the Appalachian mountains of North Carolina, she transplanted to Alaska's Chugach Mountains over twenty years ago.

JOY KENNEDY-O'NEILL teaches in the English department at Brazosport College in Lake Jackson, Texas. She volunteers with members of the Texas and National Speleological Society (NSS) to promote cave exploration, safety, and conservation; her works about such endeavors were recently awarded the Writers' League of Texas's Creative Nonfiction Fellowship. She is a longtime member of the Association for the Study of Literature and the Environment (ASLE).

DAVID LUKAS is a naturalist living on the border of Yosemite National Park, where he leads nature walks and writes about the natural world. His articles on birds and natural history have appeared in *Audubon*, *Orion*, *National Wildlife*, *BBC Magazine*, and many other magazines. Until recently, his popular column "Field Guide" was a weekly feature in the *Los Angeles Times*. His books include *Wild Birds of California* (Companion Press, 2000), *Sierra Nevada Natural History* (University of California Press, 2004), and *A Year of Watching Wildlife*, a guide to the top two hundred places in the world to see wildlife (Lonely Planet, 2009). David has also contributed natural history chapters to many Lonely Planet travel guides for places like Nova Scotia, Tanzania, and Borneo.

BILL MCKIBBEN's most recent book is *Deep Economy* (Times Books, 2007). He is the author of many other books, including *The End of Nature* (1989), the first book about global warming for a general audience. He is a scholar in environmental studies at Middlebury College, and lives simply with his family in Vermont.

JORDAN FISHER SMITH spent twenty-one years as a park ranger in California, Idaho, Wyoming, and Alaska. His magazine work has appeared in *Men's Journal*, *Backpacker*, *Orion*, the *Los Angeles Times Magazine*, and other periodicals. His nonfiction book, *Nature Noir: A Park Ranger's Patrol in the Sierra*, was a Book Sense bestseller, an

Audubon Magazine Editors' Choice, and a *San Francisco Chronicle* Best Book of 2005. He is a principal character and narrator in a 2008 documentary film about Lyme disease from Open Eye Pictures, *Under Our Skin*. He is currently working on a book about the future of American wilderness. He lives in the northern Sierra Nevada.

SUSAN LEIGH TOMLINSON is a writer and director of the Natural History and Humanities degree program in the Honors College at Texas Tech University. She has a background in the natural sciences and studio arts. Her work has appeared in *Writing on the Wind: An Anthology of West Texas Women Writers*, and in *Camas, Isotope,* and other publications. She won the 2008 *Isotope* editors' prize for her nonfiction essay "Pentimento."

WILLIAM E. TYDEMAN is an archivist in the Southwest Collection/Special Collections Library at Texas Tech University.

Poet DIANE HUETER WARNER works at the Southwest Collection/Special Collections Library where she is responsible for the James Sowell Family Collection in Literature, Community, and the Natural World, a manuscript collection that includes the papers of Barry Lopez, Rick Bass, and Pattiann Rogers, among others. She earned her PhD in creative writing from Texas Tech University. Her poems and reviews have been published in numerous literary journals.

acknowledgments

We wish to express our deep gratitude to the Office of the Provost at Texas Tech University for supporting this project.

And thank you to the editors and publishers of the journals and books in which some of these essays first appeared: "From the Ground" by Marybeth Holleman, from *Alaska Quarterly Review* (vol. 24, nos. 1 and 2, Spring/Summer 2007); "Homeland Security," from *Icons of Loss and Grace: Moments from the Natural World* by Susan Hanson (Texas Tech University Press, 2004); "In the Slipstream," from *The Hopes of Snakes and Other Tales from the Urban Landscape* by Lisa Couturier (Beacon Press, 2005); "Origin Moment," from *Tracking Desire: A Journey after Swallow-tailed Kites* by Susan Cerulean (University of Georgia Press, 2005); "Angler Girl" by Susan Leigh Tomlinson, from *Isotope* (Fall/Winter 2005); "A Day in the Park," from *Nature Noir: A Park Ranger's Patrol in the Sierra* by Jordan Fisher Smith (Houghton Mifflin, 2005).